Indygo Junction's
Needle Felting
22 Stylish Projects for Home & Fashion

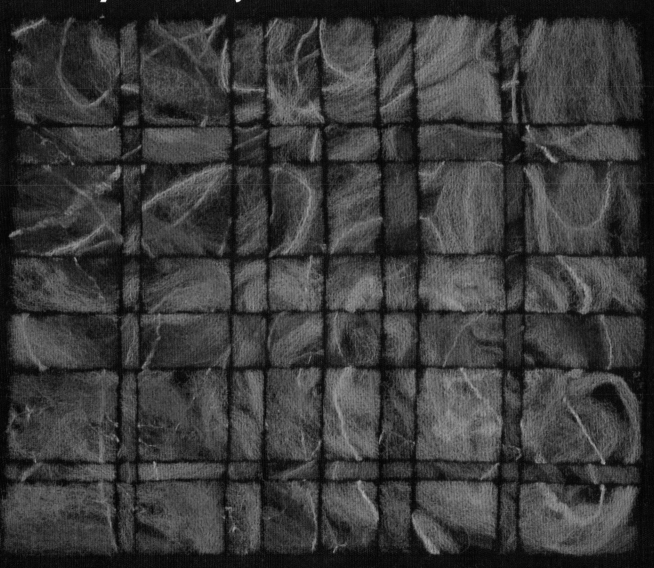

Amy Barickman

C&T PUBLISHING

Text © 2006 Amy Barickman

Artwork © 2006 C&T Publishing, Inc.

Publisher: Amy Marson

Editorial Director: Gailen Runge

Acquisitions Editor: Jan Grigsby

Editor: Candie Frankel

Technical Editors: Nanette S. Zeller, Elin Thomas

Copyeditor/Proofreader: Wordfirm Inc.

Cover Designer: Kristen Yenche

Design Director/Book Designer: Kristen Yenche

Illustrator: Kirstie L. Pettersen

Production Assistants: Zinnia Heinzmann, Matt Allen

Photography: All photography by C&T Publishing, Inc. unless otherwise noted

Published by C&T Publishing, Inc., P.O. Box 1456, Lafayette, CA 94549

Front cover: Flower Pin (top) by Barbara Lambrecht; Daylily Pin (lower right) by Diane McCauley.

Back cover: Tangled Scarf and Four Square Purse by Diane McCauley; Butterfly Pillow by Cathy Pendleton.

Library of Congress Cataloging-in-Publication Data

Barickman, Amy,

 Indygo Junction's needle felting : 22 stylish projects for home & fashion / Amy Barickman.

  p. cm.

 Includes index.

 ISBN-13: 978-1-57120-379-3 (paper trade)

 ISBN-10: 1-57120-379-6 (paper trade)

 1. Felting. 2. Felt work. I. Title: Needle felting. II. Title.

 TT849.5.B37 2006

 746'.0463--dc22   2006001457

Printed in China

10 9 8 7 6 5 4

[Handwritten annotations: 746 BAR   10/24/2012   H/LC]

ACKNOWLEDGMENTS

With thanks and appreciation to:

- The many designers who have been part of Indygo Junction through the past fifteen years. Your creative talents never cease to amaze and inspire me!

- Bob, Jack, and Emma, my husband and children, whose support and enthusiasm I cherish.

- Donna Martin, my mother and co-designer of my projects in this book, whose talents and creative inspiration have contributed to the success of Indygo Junction.

- Diane McCauley, contributor of so many beautiful projects in this collection. Your work inspired me to pursue publishing this book.

- Fellow designers Mary Ann Donze, Sarah Sporrer, Cathy Pendleton, and Leslie McCabe, who joined our creative journey and contributed valuable ideas, techniques, and designs.

- Designers Barbara Lambrecht, Suzanne Higgs, and Michele DuPont Mangham, whose work appears in the Gallery.

- Deb Rowden, who has been a fabulous coordinator and editor.

- The staff at C&T, especially Jan Grigsby, Amy Marson, Diane Pedersen, Candie Frankel, and Nanette S. Zeller.

Contents

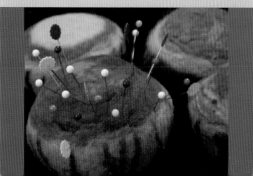

Introduction

Needle felting has ignited the creative spirit in me and in many of the designers I work with at Indygo Junction. This easy-to-learn craft allows us to create unique handmade gifts, fashion accessories, and home décor items in a short period of time. Given my busy, hectic schedule, I especially love the instant gratification needle felting affords.

This book introduces many different techniques for plying the ancient art of needle felting. Experimenting with different fibers, yarns, and foundations has been fun for all of us, and we are pleased to share our projects, including detailed instructions, with you. Meeting the farmers who shepherd the flocks that supply the wools we use was a highlight of the journey. I have a new appreciation of flocks I see in the pasture.

For those of you who love fashioning items by hand for yourself or your home, needle felting will offer you an amazing array of creative possibilities.

WHAT IS FELTING?

Wool fibers felt together because each strand of wool contains scales. The felting process causes the scales on individual fibers to lock together, forming a firm, nonraveling fabric. There are two types of felting:

Wet felting occurs when the fibers encounter heat, moisture, and abrasion, such as when you accidentally wash and dry a wool sweater.

Dry, or needle felting is the process of pushing barbed needles through layers of wool fiber or material. The fibers become firmly attached to one another without the use of sewing thread. On a much larger scale this method is used to create nonwoven materials such as craft or industrial felt.

This book focuses primarily on dry felting techniques, but does contain a few wet felting projects. Dry felting is flexible and forgiving and offers many design options. The needling can be done by hand or machine or a combination of the two.

Photo by Susan Hale, BD Photography

WHAT YOU'LL NEED

- **Fiber** Wool and natural fibers work best. We have tried needle felting with a variety of wool fibers, including merino, mohair, and corriedale wool. For the projects in this book, we suggest using sheep's wool roving. Roving from sheep's wool is readily available and inexpensive, and there is a plethora of colors. Wool blends are also available. Please note that fiber choice is personal and may vary project by project. Experimentation is part of the felting process. You are always safe using wool.

- **Yarns and Threads** Most yarns are suitable for needling. The more loosely spun the yarn, the easier it is to use. We have also needled embroidery floss and perle cotton. Experiment with different yarns and threads to find your favorites.

- **Foundation Fabric** A foundation material is used for many needle felted projects. We have experimented with many different foundations. Wool fabrics and knits, as well as shrunken wool sweaters, work really well. Wool felt, synthetic felt, denim, linen, and cotton are all good foundations.

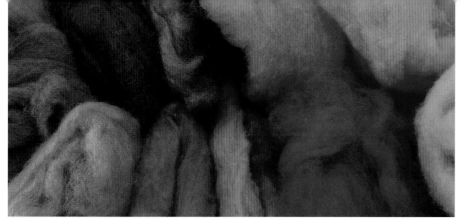

Wool roving

- **Stabilizer** We have used both water-soluble and traditional stabilizers (interfacings) as foundations for creating wool sheets and dimensional shapes such as the Daylily Pin on page 60. Choice of stabilizer is project dependent. Experiment with different types of stabilizers to achieve the desired effect.

- **Felting Needles** A felting needle is a very sharp triangular needle with downward-pointing barbs at the tip of the shaft. When the felting needle is pushed through layers of fiber or fabric, the barbs cause the scales of the fibers to enmesh and interlock. The downward point of the barbs engages the fibers when the needle is pushed into the fabric and releases the fibers when the needle is pulled out. The more the fibers are needled, the more entangled—and secured—they become. Try several needle sizes to see which works best for a particular combination of fiber or yarn and foundation fabrics.

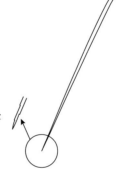

Barbed felting needle

- **Multineedle Tools** A single hand needle is wonderful for detail work, but a multineedle tool allows quicker results. Primitive screw-together wooden "ball-type" multineedle tools are available. We prefer the Clover Felting Punch Tool (see Resources), which is much more sophisticated with added features such as a spring action for effortless needling and a protective shield with locking capability for safety.

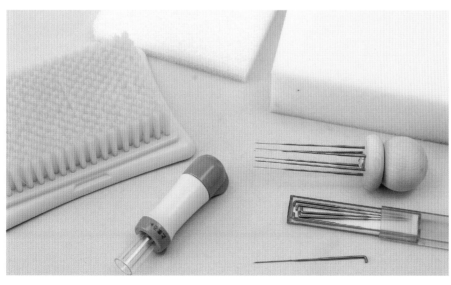

Needle felting tools

Fiber Terms

Fleece: wool directly from the animal source, before it is carded and spun into yarn.

Carded wool: wool prepared for spinning or felting. It has been run through a carding machine that brushes the wool fibers in one direction and removes knots and debris. May also be called roving.

Roving: wool that is washed, carded, and ready to be spun into yarn.

Corriedale: a high-quality wool with bright luster and a shorter fiber length. Corriedale is usually recommended for dry felting. It is similar to merino but usually less expensive.

Merino: a luxuriously soft wool that has become an industry standard for top quality. It usually has a longer fiber length and is recommended for surface embellishment and wet felting.

Mohair: yarn spun from the hair of the Angora goat and rabbit. Mohair is silky, durable, lightweight, and warm.

Needle Sizes

The size of the needle determines its function and the size of the holes left behind. Slightly rubbing or brushing a surface can reduce the appearance of needle holes. Wetting the fiber may also help reduce the size of the holes. Personal preference and fiber choices will be the ultimate determination of needle size. Use the following guide as a starting point:

36-gauge needle is used for coarse needling. This sturdy, aggressive needle works well for basting projects or for use with coarse wools or fabrics. It will leave visible holes in the fibers.

38-gauge and Clover Thick Felting Punch needles are good for all-purpose needling. They leave less visible holes and, among other applications, are useful for appliquéing one layer to another.

40-gauge and Clover Thin Felting Punch needles are good for detail needling. Because they don't leave visible holes, they work well for fine finishing. They're great for smoothing out holes left by thicker-gauge needling.

■ Work Surfaces The traditional work surface for hand needling is dense foam, approximately 2 inches thick. We, however, prefer the Clover Felting Punch Mat (see Resources), which has a brushlike work surface. The Felting Punch Mat does not wear out after repeated use and protects needles from breaking and dulling. Fibers tend to become entangled in a foam mat, which makes it difficult to remove the project from the work surface. The Felting Punch Mat allows projects to be easily pulled away after needling.

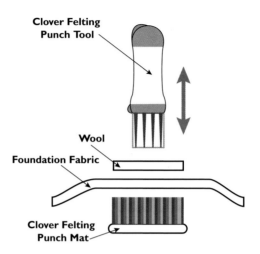

Felting wool to foundation fabric with Clover tools

■ Needle Felting Machine For faster progress with a project, needle felting can be accomplished with a dedicated machine or a special sewing machine attachment. The machine (or attachment) has a number of felting needles. The concept is the same as needle felting by hand, but the action is much faster and more aggressive. A machine is often a better choice than hand felting when combining blends and synthetic felts. Several sewing machine manufacturers (Babylock, Brother, and Bernina) offer equipment for machine needle felting. Most of the machine felted projects in this book were created with Babylock's Embellisher Machine (see Resources).

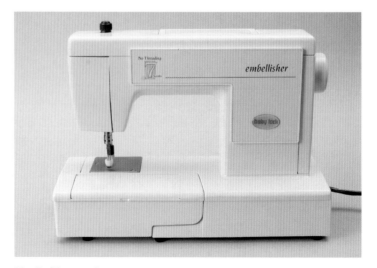

Needle felting machine

Needle Felting Tips

As you work the fibers with a felting needle, the top layer of fibers passes through to the layers below. You should periodically lift the project from the work surface to look at the reverse side of the project. This visual inspection will help you determine where the project needs more needling (top fibers are not visible on the back side) and where the fibers are secure (top fibers are visible on the back side and evenly affixed). Also known as "reverse felting," using the "wrong" side of the felt can offer a softer look to a finished project.

Depending on the foundation fabric and yarn combination, the foundation fabric may draw in, especially in areas where the needle felting is dense. To help the fabric "relax," you will want to block the project. Place the project on an ironing board and hold a steam iron above it, without actually touching the fibers with the iron. Generously steam the affected area. Then pull and stretch the foundation back into its original shape, pinning it to the ironing board if necessary. Let the project dry in that position before continuing.

Yarn Embellishment

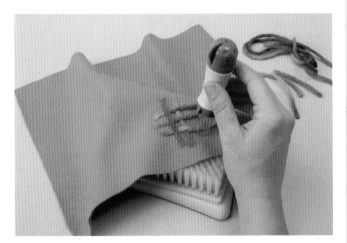

Embellish wool felt with yarn.

This dry felting technique allows you to apply yarn to a foundation fabric. It is a good introductory technique to help you become used to the stabbing motion used in needling. Choose 100% wool yarn or high wool content yarn blends. If the yarn has a slight twist, use a 36-gauge needle. For loosely twisted yarn, use either a 36- or 38-gauge needle or a Clover Thick Felting Punch tool. As you gain experience, you may wish to experiment with other types of yarns.

Begin by laying the foundation fabric on the work surface. Loosely place a few inches of yarn on the foundation in the desired pattern; avoid stretching the yarn. Tack the yarn into position with a single felting needle, stabbing here and there to loosely anchor it. You don't need to stab too deeply—about ⅛ inch to ¼ inch, or just enough for the barbs on the needle to pass through the yarn and foundation layers. Position a few more inches of yarn and continue stabbing. Continue in this manner until the yarn is roughly in place. Check the yarn position, make any final adjustments, and then stab *repeatedly* into the yarn until it is securely anchored. This may take a while, so put on some jazzy music and stab away! Using a multineedle tool makes the process go faster.

Lift the foundation fabric periodically and check the reverse side to determine where you need more needling and where the yarn is secure (see Needle Felting Tips on left).

Needle Safety

Felting needles are extremely sharp. Keep your eyes on your work and don't become distracted. Pay attention to where you are stabbing and keep your fingers clear of the active work area. Consider using latex finger protectors to guard against pokes. Safely stow the needle when it is not in use by pushing it into the work surface. The Clover Felting Punch Tool offers built-in safety with a clear plastic protective shield around the needles and a locking feature that secures the shield in place when the tool is not in use.

FABRIC TO FABRIC

Needle felt wool material to foundation fabric.

The technique of needle felting wool material to a foundation fabric allows you to appliqué without sewing. You can use purchased felt or make your own by shrinking wool yardage or old wool sweaters. The needling can be done by hand or machine.

Begin by placing the foundation fabric on the work surface. Then arrange appliqué shapes on the foundation. Needle the center of the shape to "baste" it in place. Then loosely needle around the edges of the appliqué. Finally, needle over the entire shape until it is securely anchored. For greater efficiency on larger shapes, try a multineedle tool. Another option for quick and secure appliqué felting is to use a needle felting machine or attachment. Experiment with your materials to determine your preferences.

FIBER TO FABRIC

Use patterns or work freehand to needle roving to foundation fabric.

This felting method uses patterns, outlines, and freehand techniques to attach roving to the foundation fabric. Depending on how much fiber you apply, the design may be transparent, opaque, or a combination of the two. With enough fiber, the design can even become three-dimensional. Patterns can come from a variety of sources. Start with simple shapes, such as circles, leaves, or simple flower designs.

■ **Paper Pattern** Draw or trace a design on paper and cut it out. Lay foundation fabric on the work surface. Place roving fibers on the foundation to cover an area slightly larger than the pattern piece, then place the paper pattern on top of the roving. Needle around the edge of the pattern, going up and down until the fibers have compressed and you can see the outline of the shape. Remove the paper. Fold any

How to Felt Wool Yardage and Sweaters

You can shrink 100% wool fabric and knits in a home washing machine. Start with at least double the yardage you would normally need. The amount of shrinkage will vary depending on the type of wool and the weave. Generally, you can expect wool fabric and sweaters to shrink to *approximately* half their original size. Often there is more shrinkage in the lengthwise direction than in the width.

Machine wash wool fabric in the hottest water available, using a little laundry detergent in the first wash and setting the machine for the longest agitation cycle. Keep in mind that different types of washing machines will felt differently. For additional shrinkage, dry in a hot dryer. To avoid dangerous lint buildup in your washer and dryer, wash and dry wool fabrics in an old pillowcase that has been tied closed.

Many fabrics will felt with a single wash or a wash and dry. Others will require additional wash/dry cycles. If the fabric is extremely stubborn, add a kettle or two of boiling water to the wash water and reset the agitation several times. Your goal is to shrink the wool to the point at which it will no longer ravel but not so much that it becomes too bulky and stiff.

excess fiber that extends beyond the shape back into the design and finish needling the shape. Lift your shape off the work surface to see how well the fibers have needled through the foundation (see Needle Felting Tips on page 7). Continue needling and adding fibers to create the desired look.

- **Stencil** Follow the paper pattern method above, using a stencil as a design template.

- **Yarn Outline** Use yarn to needle a design outline (see Yarn Embellishment on page 7) and then fill it in with fiber.

- **Cookie Cutters** After placing the foundation fabric on the work surface, position a cookie cutter on the fabric. Fill the interior of the cookie cutter with fiber; start conservatively— you can always add more. Needle around the inside edge of the cookie cutter and then move in toward the middle. Add more fiber in thin areas. The metal edges of the cookie cutter allow you to create a crisp, well-defined shape.

- **Freehand** Try twisting, shaping, braiding, weaving, or rolling the fiber to create a design directly on the background. Then needle it in place.

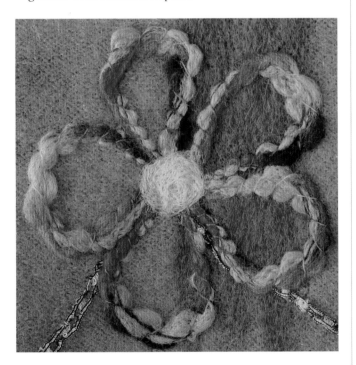

WOOL FROM SCRATCH

Needled layers of wool roving create sheets of felt.

This technique allows you to create felt fabric from scratch. You will need an ounce of fiber for every square foot of finished felt.

Pull tufts of roving fibers and lay them on the work surface in a thin layer, covering an area roughly the size of the finished felt sheet. Lay a second layer of fibers perpendicular, or crosswise, to the first layer. Continue adding thin layers of fiber. How many layers you add depends on the desired final thickness, usually $1/8$ inch. Needle through all the layers to entangle the fibers together. Use a multineedle tool or needle felting machine to cover the area quickly.

Once your sheet is securely felted, carefully remove it from the work surface. Turn the felt sheet over and gently needle any loose fibers on the back side. You may have to work and turn your sheet several times to obtain a smooth finish. Hold the sheet up to the light to check for thin areas. Needle extra fiber into these areas to create a uniform thickness.

Now that you know the basics, you're ready to begin. Follow our instructions to make 22 unique projects. Browse through our Gallery for even more project ideas. Enjoy!

Yarn Embellishment

CONFETTI JACKET

 by Diane McCauley

This cheerful jacket uses three embellishment techniques on the lapels, cuffs, back belt, and edging. Machine needle felting is suggested because surface areas this large would take a long time to complete by hand. Yarn edging is also more manageable by machine.

SUPPLIES

Jacket pattern (IJ725 One Button Swing Topper by Mary Ann Donze from Indygo Junction, Inc.)

$1\frac{1}{2}$ to $1\frac{5}{8}$ yards medium or heavyweight wool felt or tightly woven, nonraveling wool, 60″ wide

Wool roving, up to $\frac{1}{2}$ oz. each of four colors: red, blue, yellow, and lime green

Variety of tapestry wool or other fine wool yarn in five colors: red, blue, yellow, medium yellow-green, and turquoise

16 yards novelty variegated fuzzy yarn (Bernat, *Frenzy*, Racy Red)

Matching sewing thread

Tailor's chalk

Needle felting tools

INSTRUCTIONS

Refer to Yarn Embellishment on page 7 and Fiber to Fabric on page 8. To make the jacket as shown, use View 4 of the Indygo Junction pattern and add the back belt from View 3. Needle felt the belt and cuffs during Step 2. Needle felt the lapels and collar in Step 5.

1. Make jacket pattern alterations as needed. Cut out all the fabric pieces, eliminating facings and hems and adjusting for shrinkage.

Will It Shrink?

Needle felting shrinks some fabrics. Before cutting out the garment pieces that will be needle felted, test your embellishment technique on a 4″ × 4″ scrap of garment fabric. If the scrap still measures 4″ × 4″ after embellishing, then cut your pieces to match the patterns. If the embellished scrap measures less than 4″ × 4″, cut the pieces larger than the patterns and trim to size after embellishing.

2. Add needle felted embellishment to cuffs and belt piece using the following techniques:

Multicolor background Arrange small amounts of roving in a random pattern on the fabric. Don't cover the entire surface; keep it light to allow some of the garment fabric to show through. Needle felt lightly to hold in position.

Confetti Cut $\frac{1}{4}$″ to $\frac{3}{8}$″ lengths of tapestry yarn in several colors. Scatter cut yarn over surface of felted roving, avoiding clumps. Needle felt in place.

Block belt and cuffs if necessary (see Needle Felting Tips on page 7).

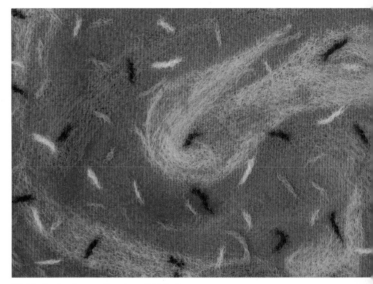

Multicolor background and confetti patterns.

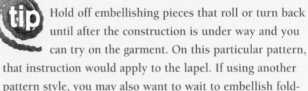 Hold off embellishing pieces that roll or turn back until after the construction is under way and you can try on the garment. On this particular pattern, that instruction would apply to the lapel. If using another pattern style, you may also want to wait to embellish fold-back cuffs or certain collar styles. Your body type will affect how the lapel or collar rolls, and your arm length will determine the fold line of the cuff.

3. Place fuzzy variegated novelty yarn along the edges of the cuff and belt embellishment and needle felt in place. Repeat on reverse side. Trim the cuff fabric close to the yarn edging.

4. Sew the jacket, following the pattern instructions and eliminating facings and hems. For less bulk and a more finished appearance, lap the seams: overlap the fabric pieces, right sides up and seamlines matching. Stitch along the seamline and again $1/4''$ away. Trim the excess fabric close to the stitching on both sides.

 Lapped seams work well on straight or slightly curved seams. They are less successful on deep curves, such as underarm seams. Within a single garment, seam types may be mixed.

5. Try on the jacket and use chalk to mark the lapel roll lines; blend line into back collar seam. Use the marked lines as a guide for working the multicolor background and confetti embellishment (Step 2) on the lapels and back collar. On the lower, tapered end of a turned-back lapel, needle felt up to the roll line only. If the needle felting extends beyond the roll line, the reverse side of felting will show on the front of the garment. You can be less exact higher up on the lapel or in areas where the wrong side of the needle felting will not show. If necessary, block felted areas of garment.

6. Place fuzzy variegated novelty yarn along the outer edges of hem, lapel, and collar and needle felt in place. Repeat on reverse side of the garment. Trim the garment fabric close to the yarn edging.

Needle felt novelty yarn to outer edges of jacket.

Optional: If the edges of the garment fabric are prone to fraying, sew a medium zigzag stitch or serge very close to the edge. If the fuzzies on the inside back neck are uncomfortable, line this area with a scrap of lightweight silky fabric cut on the bias. Turn under the edges and hand sew in place.

More Design Ideas

Experiment with other allover felted embellishment patterns. Try squiggles, straight or wavy stripes, or crisscrossed lines to create your own custom plaid.

Use needle felting to fake a yoke or other construction detail. Mark the detailing area on the garment piece, needle felt within the marked area, and edge with a matching or contrasting yarn to simulate two separate pieces.

 by Diane McCauley

The idea for this 4″ × 67″ scarf was born when a badly behaved dog got into a ball of yarn. Long and skinny with open work, this scarf is a stylish lightweight accessory. Try it with a jeans jacket or to dress down a more formal jacket. Our designer needle felted by machine.

SUPPLIES

Felted wool, 6″ × 70″ (or desired length + 3″)

18 to 20 yards extra-bulky variegated wool yarn with little or no twist to resemble pencil roving (double the yardage if a less bulky yarn is used)

Tailor's chalk

Needle felting tools

INSTRUCTIONS

Refer to Yarn Embellishment on page 7.

1. Lay a strand of yarn on the felted wool foundation in a random, wavy design, at least 1″ from the foundation edge. If you prefer, use chalk to loosely mark a wavy pattern to use as a guide.

2. Needle felt the yarn in place. The yarn should measure ¼″ to ⅜″ wide after needle felting. If necessary, add a second row of yarn alongside the first to obtain sufficient width.

3. Repeat Steps 1 and 2 on the opposite edge of the foundation.

4. Position four or five additional lengths and colors of yarn to loosely fill the 4″-wide center of the foundation. Randomly curve and overlap yarns along the entire length of the foundation, as shown in the photographs. Make sure all the yarns are felted securely and then trim away any excess yarn.

5. Use sharp scissors to trim the foundation close to the outermost yarn on each long outside edge. Be careful not to clip into the yarn.

6. To shape the scarf ends, select two or three points at each end where the yarns meet. Trim away the foundation close to the felted yarn.

Trim off excess foundation to shape ends.

7. For scarf openwork, select and mark unembellished areas of the scarf foundation. Strive for an even balance of open-work throughout the scarf. With small, sharp scissors, cut a slit in the middle of each marked area of the foundation. Insert scissors into slit and trim close to the yarn edges to create an opening.

Cut close to yarn edges to create openwork.

 by Diane McCauley

Everyone needs at least one fun, funky purse. This little gem is made of felt, yarn, and extra-heavy interfacing. The finished size is 9½″ × 3½″ × 3½″ deep. The seam allowances are sewn on the outside for added detail. Once you understand the construction technique, you'll be able to vary the size and shape to suit your personal taste. Our designer needle felted this project by machine, but it could also be done by hand.

SUPPLIES

²⁄₃ yard wool felt, 60″ wide

6 to 8 yards assorted variegated or novelty yarns

¹⁄₃ yard heavy interfacing, 22″ wide (Timtex or Peltex Extra Firm)

¹⁄₈ yard fusible fleece

Size 90 or jeans sewing machine needle (optional)

Button, approximately 1″ diameter

Matching sewing thread and needle

Awl or seam ripper (optional)

Tailor's chalk

Needle felting tools

CUTTING

From wool felt, cut:

2 pieces 4″ × 52″, for handles

2 pieces 10¹⁄₂″ × 16″, for purse interior and exterior

From interfacing, cut and label:

1 piece, 9³⁄₄″ × 3″, for front

2 pieces, 9³⁄₄″ × 3¹⁄₄″, for bottom and back

1 piece, 9¹⁄₂″ × 3¹⁄₄″, for top

1 piece, 9¹⁄₂″ × 1¹⁄₂″, for flap

INSTRUCTIONS

Refer to Yarn Embellishment on page 7.

1. Use chalk or a pin to mark the center of one 4″ × 52″ piece of wool felt. At the center, mark 1″ in from each long side edge. Mark 4″ from each short edge. Use pencil or chalk to draw curved lines along each long edge, starting at the 4″ mark and curving in toward the corresponding 1″ mark at the center. Cut on the drawn lines to make a tapered handle. Place the tapered handle on the second 4″ × 52″ felt piece and pin. Trim the second piece to match.

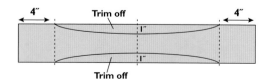

Mark and trim to create tapered handle.

2. Place 10¹⁄₂″ × 16″ purse interior and exterior pieces flat on work table. Starting from short side, use chalk to mark four 3¹⁄₂″ segments, as shown, on each piece. The last segment, purse flap, will measure 2″ from edge. Set purse interior aside until Step 5.

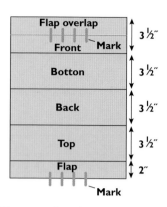

Measure and mark purse segments.

3. To create a seamless look to yarn embellishment, roll purse exterior so flap overlaps front segment. On both segments, add 4 aligned chalk marks to use as overlap placement guides. Overlap placement guides will designate where felted yarn will appear to meet at flap closure of completed purse.

Felted yarns appear to meet at overlapped flap closure.

4. Place the yarn on the purse exterior in a random, wavy pattern. On flap and front segments align yarn with placement guides, providing a seamless wrapped look. Leave a loop at the middle of the flap for the button. Securely needle felt the yarn to the

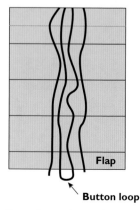

Create button loop with yarn.

purse exterior. Needle felt a similar design on one tapered purse handle.

 If your yarn is not strong enough to make an effective button loop, use elastic cord instead. Trap the cord loop between the layers in Step 5 of the assembly.

5. Place the unembellished purse interior marked side up on worktable. Position interfacing pieces on corresponding segments, as shown. Allow approximately $1/8"$ gaps between interfacing pieces and segment lines. Center interfacing pieces side to side within each segment, approximately $3/8"$ from all outside edges. So that the purse closure lays flat and smooth, top and flap interfacing were cut shorter than other interfacing pieces and will center approximately $1/2"$ from each side edge of segment. Pin interfacing in place and machine baste 2" from each long edge.

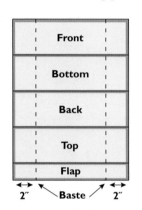

Machine baste 2" from edges.

 Some sewing machines may have difficulty sewing through thick layers of felt and interfacing. Switching to a size 90 or jeans needle may improve the performance of your machine.

6. Align purse exterior (embellished side up) on top of purse interior (interfacing side up), sandwiching the interfacing between the two felt layers. Pin. Define each segment by stitching between interfacing gaps. Press the point of an awl or seam ripper directly in front of the needle. A small valley will form between the interfaced segments to guide your stitching. Stop and restart stitching when crossing decorative trim.

7. With pencil or chalk, trace the unembellished purse handle onto fusible fleece. Trim fleece a generous $1/4"$ *inside* traced line. Center the fleece on the unembellished handle. Fuse in place.

8. Align embellished handle (right side up) on top of unembellished handle (fleece side up), sandwiching the fleece between the two layers. Stitch $1/4"$ around all edges.

9. Pin the handle to the bottom segment of the purse body, wrong sides together. (Note: seams will be on outside of purse.) Match the intersections of the stitching lines, as shown by the dots in the illustration below. With $1/4"$ seam allowance, stitch from dot to dot, backstitching to secure at each end. Repeat for the other side of the handle.

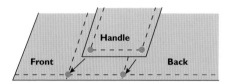

Match intersections of stitched lines, as shown by dots.

10. Clip to the dot through both purse body and handle layers. Pin the back segment of the purse to the purse handle, wrong sides together. Using a $1/4"$ seam allowance and folding the purse out of the way where necessary, stitch from the bottom dot to the top of the back segment. Backstitch securely at the top edge. Repeat for the front segment of the purse and other side of handle.

11. Remove basting. Trim all exposed seam allowances to a consistent width. Sew button to front segment. Fold front to form flap overlap.

 ■ Once the purse body is sandwiched (Step 6), add machine stitching with decorative threads. Stitching through all three layers gives a very dimensional, quilted appearance and dresses up the interior, too.

■ If you plan to heavily needle felt the purse body or handle, cut pieces 1" larger on all sides. Trim them to the correct size after needle felting to allow for any "drawing up" of the foundation fabric.

■ If a bit of interfacing or fleece extends into the seam allowance and shows when the seams are trimmed, carefully trim away as much as possible. Use a matching color permanent marker to color in anything that still shows.

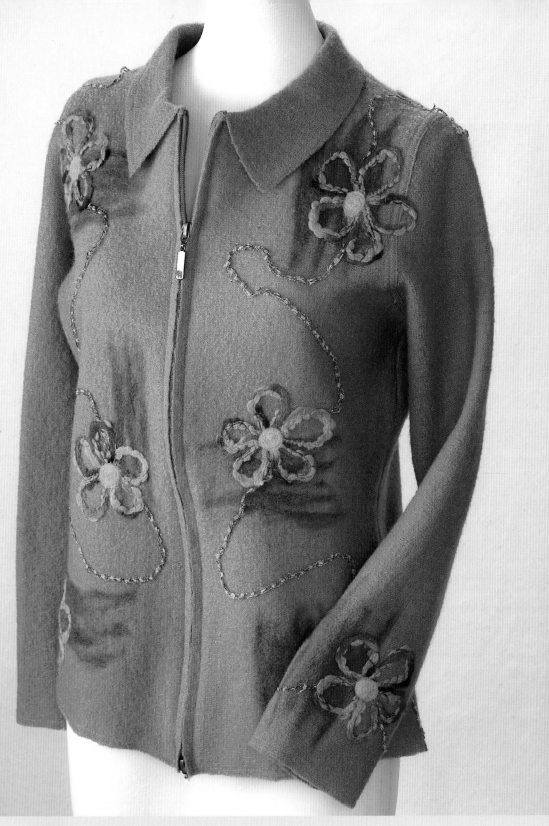

FLOWER POWER JACKET

by Diane McCauley

Use just a bit of yarn and a touch of roving to add a bevy of flowers to a new or gently worn jacket. Choose your own color palette for a custom boutique look. Our designer needle felted this jacket by machine, but it could be easily needle felted by hand.

SUPPLIES

Boiled wool jacket

18 yards loosely twisted thick-n-thin variegated wool yarn

10 yards novelty yarn, coordinated with jacket

½ oz. wool roving, for patches

½ oz. wool roving, for flower centers

Tailor's chalk

Needle felting tools

INSTRUCTIONS

Refer to Yarn Embellishment on page 7 and Fiber to Fabric on page 8.

1. Remove any patch pockets from the jacket and any buttons that could interfere with the needle felted flowers (set the buttons aside to reattach later).

2. Use chalk or pins to mark the center placement positions for 6 flowers on the jacket front (3 on each side), varying the placements. Mark the center placement for 3 flowers on the shoulder area of the jacket back. Mark the center for a flower on one or both sleeves.

3. Needle felt a very light, irregular patch of roving near each center placement mark, allowing some of the jacket fabric to show through the fibers. Vary the length, width, and direction of each roving patch, as shown in the photograph.

4. Starting at the bottom of one side seam, lay the novelty yarn on the jacket. With a felting needle, baste the yarn loosely up the jacket front, looping and curving from one flower center to another. Continue looping the yarn around the back shoulders and back down the other side of the jacket front, ending at the side seam. Needle felt yarn to secure it in place. Repeat around sleeve(s), beginning and ending yarn at the flower center.

5. With chalk, align and mark the flower pattern (page 73) at each center placement position. Overlap the pattern on the patches needle felted in Step 3.

6. Position a segment of thick-n-thin yarn along the marked flower pattern so that the thickest area of the yarn falls at the outer end of a petal. Needle felt the petal in place and trim away excess yarn. In the same manner, needle felt four more petals to complete the flower. Strive to make the petals similar in size, but for visual interest do *not* make them identical. Repeat for all marked flowers.

Needle felt petals in place, overlapping roving patches.

7. Twist a narrow length of roving and form it into a spiral for the flower center. Needle felt in place. Repeat for each flower.

8. Check the jacket for any area that looks drawn or pulled. Block distorted areas as necessary (see Needle Felting Tips on page 7).

9. Reattach buttons, if necessary.

 tip For a design that is less bold, embellish a limited area of the jacket, such as the collar, yoke, or cuffs, or choose a design with smaller flowers.

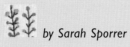 *by Sarah Sporrer*

You can needle felt into fibers other than wool. This folk art quilt has a 100% cotton background. We felted the design by hand in the same manner as we would with wool. The finished size is 17½″ × 33″.

SUPPLIES

Yardages are based on 40″-wide fabric (after prewashing).

Cotton fabrics:

 1 fat quarter for vase

 ³⁄₈ yard for background

 ¹⁄₄ yard for inner border

 1 yard for outer border, binding, and backing

Low-loft batting, 21¹⁄₂″ × 37″

Assorted yarns: dark green, red, and pink-red

Matching sewing thread; black and matching quilting thread and needles

Tailor's chalk

Needle felting tools

CUTTING

From vase fabric, cut:
1 vase pattern (page 76); for turned-under appliqué, trim ¹⁄₈″ outside pattern line

From background fabric, cut:
1 background 9¹⁄₂″ × 25″

From inner border fabric, cut:
2 side inner border strips 2″ × 25″

2 top and bottom inner border strips 2″ × 12¹⁄₂″

From outer border fabric, cut:
2 side outer border strips 3″ × 28″

2 top and bottom outer border strips 3″ × 17¹⁄₂″

1 backing 21¹⁄₂″ × 37″

INSTRUCTIONS

Refer to Yarn Embellishment on page 7.

1. Place the vase on background 1″ from bottom edge and centered side to side. Appliqué in place with black quilting thread and straight stitch.

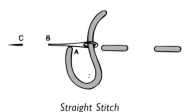

Straight Stitch

2. With chalk, mark part or all of the berries pattern (page 76) on the background. Place lengths of dark green yarn on the background for the long and short stems. Needle felt in place.

3. Place a strip of red or pink yarn on the end of a short stem. Curl yarn into a circle and felt in place. Repeat for each berry.

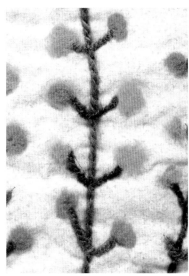

Curl yarn into a circle and felt in place.

4. Using a ¹⁄₄″ seam allowance, sew side inner border strips to background. Press toward borders. Add top and bottom inner borders. Press.

5. Sew side outer border strips to the quilt top. Press toward outer borders. Add top and bottom outer borders. Press.

6. Place the quilt backing right side down on work table. Layer batting, then quilt top, right side up, on backing. Smooth the layers and pin. Hand quilt short, even stitches around the vase, through the center of each stem, and next to the inner and outer border seam allowances.

7. Trim the backing ³⁄₄″ larger than quilt top on all sides. Trim batting close to edges of quilt top. Form binding by double-folding edges of backing onto front of quilt top and hand sewing into place.

Fabric to Fabric

 by Amy Barickman

What fun you will have combining different fabrics and yarns for this scarf. The fabric is torn to size to create soft, textured edges and then joined by machine felting. The embellishments are needle felted by hand. The finished scarf is 8″ × 67″.

SUPPLIES

Yardages are based on 16″ × 26″ fat quarter cuts.

Wool fabric (Weeks Dye Works, color Bubble Gum, patterns):

1 fat quarter solid

1 fat quarter houndstooth

1 fat quarter herringbone

Variegated, mixed fiber yarn

Matching sewing thread

Tailor's chalk

Needle felting tools

CUTTING

From solid, tear or cut:
2 pieces 8″ × 14″

From houndstooth, tear or cut:
2 pieces 8″ × 14″

From herringbone, tear or cut:
1 piece 8″ × 14″

INSTRUCTIONS

Refer to Yarn Embellishment on page 7 and Fabric to Fabric on page 8.

1. With chalk, trace pattern shapes (page 75) at least 1″ apart on remaining uncut wool fabric. Mark shape outline for 9 petals on solid, 4 petals on houndstooth, and 3 leaves and 3 flower centers on herringbone.

2. Place yarn on marked outlines and needle felt in place. Trim foundation of leaves and flower centers close to felted yarn. Trim petals ⅛″ from felted yarn.

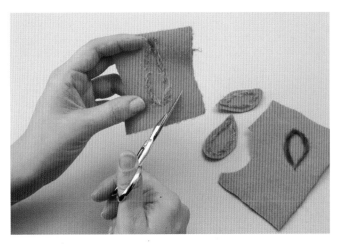

Trim petals ⅛″ from felted yarn.

3. Arrange 8″ × 14″ fabric pieces end to end, as follows: solid, houndstooth, herringbone, solid, houndstooth. Overlap short ends ¾″ and needle felt to join. Secure each join with machine zigzag stitches using matching thread.

4. Referring to the photograph, arrange the flower pieces— petals, leaves, then flower centers—on the scarf. Keep pieces at least 2″ from bottom edge to allow for fringe. Pin in place.

5. Place yarn for vines on one end of scarf. Needle felt yarn in place. Needle felt the petals, leaves, and flower centers, removing the pins just before you work each piece.

6. Draw out threads at each end of the scarf to fringe edges. Zigzag the edges to secure the weave.

GO FISH PILLOW

by Cathy Pendleton

Every mountain lake lodge needs a pillow like this. We used an intensive machine felting technique. Hand felting is possible, but machine felting works better for blends that contain less wool. Appliqué is another way to add the fish design. Experiment to see which technique works best for you to complete this 12″ × 18″ pillow.

SUPPLIES

Yardages are based on 36″-wide fabric (unwashed).

Wool felt (National Nonwovens colors):

½ yard Slate

Vineyard, 9″ × 12″

Cloudy Day, 9″ × 12″

Purple Heart, 9″ × 12″

Red and off-white perle cotton

Embroidery needle, size #22

Matching or neutral sewing thread and needle

Black quilting thread

Fiberfill

Needle felting tools

CUTTING

Use the fish patterns on page 72.

From Slate, cut:

1 backing, 12½″ × 18½″

1 upper fin and 1 lower fin

2 background blocks, 5″ × 8″

2 border strips, 2″ × 9½″

2 border strips, 2″ × 18½″

From Vineyard, cut:

1 fish head

2 background blocks, 5″ × 8″

From Cloudy Day, cut:

3 fish gills

1 foundation, 6″ × 9″

From Purple Heart, cut:

1 fish body

INSTRUCTIONS

Refer to Fabric to Fabric on page 8.

1. Center fish body and fish head on foundation. Slip the fins under the body, using fin underlaps as a guide. Needle felt pieces to foundation by machine. Add gills and needle felt in place.

2. With off-white perle cotton, hand embroider stars and French knots on felted foundation.

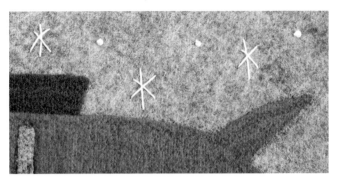

Hand embroider stars and French knots on background with perle cotton.

3. Arrange the four background blocks as shown. Sew the pieces together in pairs using a ¼″ seam allowance and matching or neutral thread. Press seams open. Cross-stitch the seamlines with red perle cotton.

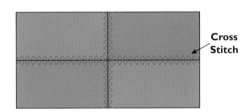

Cross-stitch seamlines with red perle cotton.

4. Center fish-embellished foundation on pieced background. Appliqué in place with black quilting thread and blanket stitch.

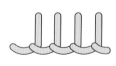

Blanket Stitch

5. With ¼″ seam allowance, sew one 2″ × 9½″ border strip to each side of background. Press seams open. Sew one 2″ × 18½″ border strip to top and one to bottom. Press seams open to complete pillow front.

6. Align pillow front and backing, right sides facing. Stitch with ¼″ seam allowance all around pillow, leaving a 3″ opening. Turn right side out. Stuff with fiberfill and sew the opening closed.

 by Cathy Pendleton

This 12″ × 12″ decorative pillow was made using the same methods as the Go Fish Pillow on page 24. Collect funky trims to add interest and make your pillow unique. Consider using different wools to complement your designs.

SUPPLIES

Yardages are based on 36″-wide fabric (unwashed).

Wool felt (National Nonwovens colors)

   ½ yard Slate

   Lemongrass, 9″ × 12″

   Cucumber Crush, 9″ × 12″

   Vineyard, 9″ × 12″

   Blue Spruce, 9″ × 12″

¾ yard fringe trim

Off-white perle cotton

Matching or neutral sewing thread

Black quilting thread

Embroidery needle, size #22

Fiberfill

Needle felting tools

CUTTING

Use the butterfly patterns on page 76.

From Slate, cut:

1 foundation, 5″ × 5″

2 border strips, 2″ × 9½″

2 border strips, 2″ × 12½″

1 backing, 12½″ × 12½″

From Lemongrass, cut:

2 background blocks, 5″ × 5″

From Cucumber Crush, cut:

1 butterfly body

2 background blocks, 5″ × 5″

From Vineyard, cut:

1 left and 1 right upper wing

From Blue Spruce, cut:

1 left and 1 right lower wing

2 antennae tips

INSTRUCTIONS

Refer to Fabric to Fabric on page 8.

1. Center butterfly body on foundation. Slip lower wings (left and right) under the body, using lower wing underlap as a guide. Position upper wings over lower wings, but under body, using upper wing underlap as a guide. Needle felt all the pieces by machine. Add the antennae tips and needle felt in place.

2. Hand embroider the antennae using off-white perle cotton.

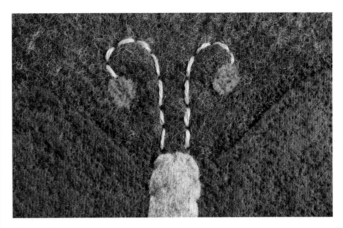

Hand embroider antennae.

3. Arrange the four background blocks, as shown, to create a four-patch design. Sew the pieces together in pairs using a ¼″ seam allowance and matching or neutral thread. Press seams open.

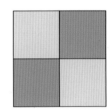

Sew blocks together using ¼″ seam allowance.

4. Center the butterfly embellished foundation on four-patch background. Slip fringe underneath the foundation edges. Appliqué foundation and fringe in place with black quilting thread and blanket stitch.

Blanket Stitch

5. With ¼″ seam allowance, sew one 2″ × 9½″ border strip to each side of background. Press seams open. Sew one 2″ × 12½″ border strip to top and one to bottom. Press seams to complete pillow front.

6. Align pillow front and backing, right sides facing. Stitch, with ¼″ seam allowance all around pillow, leaving a 3″ opening. Turn right side out. Stuff with fiberfill and sew the opening closed.

PEARS TABLE MAT

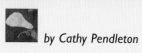

by Cathy Pendleton

To enrich the color palette of this 11″ × 24″ mat, try blending wools to create your own custom felts. Look for unconventional ways to add zesty accents, such as blending in cosmetics, crayons, or oil pastels. Felt this piece by machine or by hand.

SUPPLIES

Yardages are based on 36″-wide fabric (unwashed).

Wool felt (National Nonwovens colors)

³⁄₄ yard Slate

Hay Bale, 9″ × 12″

Ember, 9″ × 12″

Olive, 3″ × 3″

Scrap of Chestnut

¹⁄₂ yard green wool yarn

Black and matching quilting thread and needle

Cosmetic blush for shading

Compass

Needle felting tools

CUTTING

Use the pear patterns on pages 72 and 73. Use a compass to draw circles.

From Slate, cut:
1 table mat, 11″ × 24″

1 backing, 12¹⁄₂″ × 25¹⁄₂″

From Hay Bale, cut:
1 small pear

1 curved pear

From Ember, cut:
2 large pears

1 small circle, 4¹⁄₂″

From Olive, cut:
4 leaf A

2 leaf B

1 large circle, 6¹⁄₂″

From Chestnut, cut:
4 pear stems

INSTRUCTIONS

Refer to Yarn Embellishment on page 7 and Fabric to Fabric on page 8.

1. Place one small or curved pear and one large pear on each end of 11″ × 24″ table mat; keep pears at least 2¹⁄₂″ from edges. Slip end of a stem under the top of each pear. Needle felt all the pieces in place. Arrange leaves on table mat and needle felt in place.

2. Arrange small strips of yarn on felted table mat to form curling tendrils at each pear. Needle felt tendrils in place.

3. Place large circle, centered, on table mat. Appliqué in place with black thread and blanket stitch. Center small circle on large circle and appliqué.

Appliqué circles onto table mat.

4. Shade lighter colored pears with cosmetic blush to add dimension.

5. Center the table mat on backing. Baste layers together and hand quilt with matching thread, through all layers around the pears, leaves, and circles.

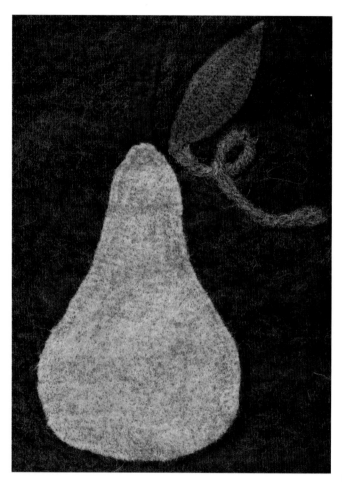

Hand quilt around pears, leaves, and circles.

6. Clip each corner of backing diagonally. Fold the backing edges onto the front of the table mat and stitch in place, forming a miter at each corner.

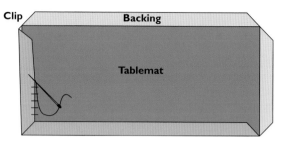

Clip backing at each corner; fold forward and stitch to create binding.

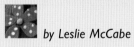 *by Leslie McCabe*

Can we ever really have enough flowers? Joining layers of felt together lets you determine the thickness of this fun pin. We created our flower with machine needle felting. Add your own beads, buttons, and extra embellishments and enjoy wearing it on your lapel! Finished size approximately 3½″ in diameter.

SUPPLIES

Red wool felt, 10″ × 10″

Small quantities of wool roving in three colors: white, black, gold

Pin back

Matching thread and needle or glue

Needle felting tools

INSTRUCTIONS

Refer to Fabric to Fabric and Fiber to Fabric on page 8.

1. Cut 2 flower patterns (page 75) from wool felt.

2. Layer felt flowers pieces together, aligning edges. Needle felt to join layers together.

3. Needle felt small pieces of white roving to the petals to form white dots.

4. Roll a ¼″ ball of gold roving. Place it on the center of the flower and needle felt in place.

5. Needle felt a narrow ring of black roving around the flower center.

6. Sew or glue pin back to the back of flower.

Fiber to Fabric

by Amy Barickman

Bring these lovely flowers to life when you needle felt by hand. Add shading and let some flowers fade into the background. We show this design as a pillow, but it could also work as a wallhanging. The finished size is 15″ × 17″.

SUPPLIES

Yardages are based on 16″ × 26″ fat quarter cuts.

Wool fabric (Weeks Dye Works, color Kudzu, patterns)

1 fat quarter solid

1 fat quarter houndstooth

2 yards variegated thick-n-thin yarn (Cascade Yarns, Jazz)

Matching or neutral sewing thread and needle

Fiberfill

Needle felting tools

CUTTING

From solid, cut:
1 pillow front, 12″ × 14″

From houndstooth, cut:
1 pillow back, 15″ × 17″

1 vase (page 74)

INSTRUCTIONS

Refer to Fabric to Fabric and Fiber to Fabric on page 8.

1. Place the vase on pillow front 3¼″ from bottom edge. Needle felt around edges of vase. Leave mouth of vase open to insert stems.

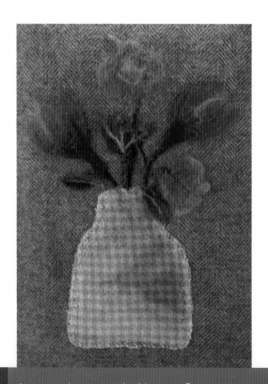

2. Cut several 2″ to 4″ pieces of thick-n-thin yarn in assorted shades. Twist the lower end of each piece to make a stem. Fan out the fibers at the top to form thistlelike flowers. Spread some flowers open and leave others compact.

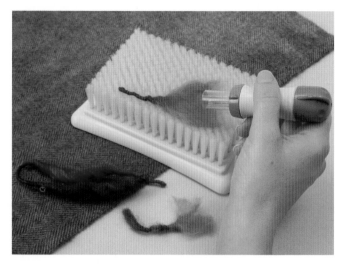

Fan fibers to form thistlelike flowers.

3. Arrange the flowers on pillow front, darker colors toward the bottom and center. Insert the stems into vase opening. Loosely needle felt by hand, basting pieces in place.

4. Cut a few 1″ to 2″ lengths of yarn for leaves. Twist yarn tightly, then slightly open middle of twist to create leaf shapes. Shade with thin strips of lighter fibers to suggest veining. Add the leaves to the composition. Loosely needle felt to baste.

5. Needle felt the design by hand or machine. Add more yarn roving to shade the flowers and vein the leaves. Needle felt the mouth of the vase closed.

6. Center pillow front on pillow back, wrong sides facing. Needle felt or sew by hand or machine around the edge of the pillow front to secure the pieces together. Lay yarn roving over the joined edges and needle felt in place.

7. Cut a 3″ to 4″ slit in center of pillow back. Stuff with fiberfill and whipstitch closed.

 by Amy Barickman

Gear up your imagination to finish the edges of these funky mittens. Leave the seams raw, pink them, fray them, or stitch together flat, as shown. We experimented with both hand and machine felting and found that machine felting works better with the wool-blend felt used in this project. Your mittens will be warm and oh so fashion forward!

SUPPLIES

Yardages are based on 36˝-wide fabric (unwashed).

Wool felt (National Nonwovens colors):

¼ yard Vineyard or Olive

¼ yard Berries & Cream or Cedar Chest

¼ yard Amethyst or Butterscotch

Wool roving, up to ½ oz. each of 2 or 3 coordinating colors (National Nonwovens Shaded Wisps)

Matching or neutral sewing thread

Needle felting tools

CUTTING

Use the mitten patterns on page 73.

From Vineyard or Olive, cut:
1 mitten back and 1 reverse mitten back

From Berries & Cream or Cedar Chest, cut:
1 mitten upper palm and 1 reverse mitten upper palm

From Amethyst or Butterscotch, cut:
1 mitten lower palm and 1 reverse mitten lower palm

INSTRUCTIONS

Refer to Fiber to Fabric on page 8.

1. From assorted colors of roving, cut six 12˝ strips and twelve 7˝ strips. Roll the roving to compress and flatten slightly. Place 3 long roving strips on each mitten back, aligning vertically and spacing 1⅛˝ to 1¼˝ apart.

2. Weave 6 short strips, placed horizontally and evenly spaced, over and under the long strips on each mitten back to create a plaid pattern. Needle felt to secure fibers in place.

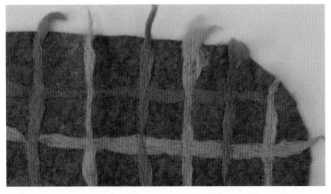

Weave short strips over long strips to create plaid pattern.

 tip Slight dampening helps hold roving fibers together, especially when using blends with high synthetic content. Use a wet sponge or the fine mist from a spray bottle to dampen the fibers. Allow fibers to dry before needling.

3. With ¼˝ seam allowance, stitch an upper palm to its matching lower palm, right sides together. Align each mitten back with its corresponding palm, right sides together. Stitch with ¼˝ seam allowance all around edges, leaving the wrist edge open. Turn right side out.

 tip Creative edging effects can be made by sewing the mitten backs and palms together with right sides facing out, so no turning is required after stitching. Edges of seam allowance may be left raw, pinked, or frayed.

4. Flatten some roving to make a 1¼˝-wide strip. Apply the roving to the inside wrist of the mitten, letting it extend ¾˝ beyond the raw edge. Needle felt in place. Fold the roving around the raw edge onto the outside of the mitten and needle felt to secure.

Needle felt roving onto raw edge of wrist.

 by Diane McCauley

The secret to these perfectly formed wool roving dots is a round cookie cutter. Add a flirty fringe of felted buttons and you have a scarf unlike any other. The scarf measures 7″ × 57″ and is needle felted by hand.

SUPPLIES

¼ yard high wool content felt, 60″ wide (Moda wool-blend felt, color 1702-28)

½ oz. wool roving

¾″-diameter round cookie cutter (or substitute)

#5 perle cotton to match roving

Embroidery needle, size #22

Sewing thread to match wool felt and needle

Needle felting tools

> **tip** Look for small, round cookie cutters in kitchen supply or cake decorating stores or in the clay section of your local craft store. A homemade alternative is a rigid plastic lid from a pump spray bottle (such as a hair spray container). Use utility scissors or a knife to cut the top off the lid.

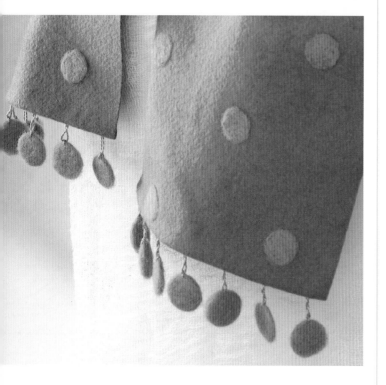

INSTRUCTIONS

Refer to Fiber to Fabric on page 8.

1. Cut the wool felt evenly to make a piece 7″ × 60″. Trim off both selvages.

2. Lay the wool felt foundation on work surface. Set the cookie cutter in a desired location on the foundation. Press the cutter down firmly and fill with roving. Stab the roving with a single felting needle until it is evenly distributed and loosely anchored (10 to 12 stabs). Do not remove the cutter.

Use small cookie cutter and roving to form spots.

3. Hold the needle directly against the inside edge of the cutter and poke repeatedly along the edge to clearly define the dot. Then needle felt in toward the center of the dot. Fill in any voids or lightly covered areas with more roving and needle felting.

> **tip** Practice making a few polka dots on scrap fabric to get a feel for how much roving is needed. Strive to use equal amounts of roving for each dot.

4. Remove cutter. Continue needle felting dot until firmly anchored, taking care not to disturb or distort the outer edges. Repeat Steps 2–4 for each dot, spacing the dots 2″ apart or as desired.

5. Use the cookie cutter and remaining roving to make 14 wet felted buttons (see Felted Buttons on page 57).

6. Fold short edge of scarf ¼" to the wrong side and press. Using a ruler and chalk, start ½" from one side and make seven marks 1" apart along the folded edge.

7. Draw two parallel lines 8" long and ½" apart on a piece of paper. Align the folded edge of the scarf wrong side up on one line. Pin in place.

8. Thread embroidery needle with 1½ yards of perle cotton. Knot one end. Insert the needle inside the folded edge and draw it out at the first mark. Take a small stitch through the felted button. Hold the edge of the button even with the upper pencil line on the paper and make a knot in the button as illustrated.

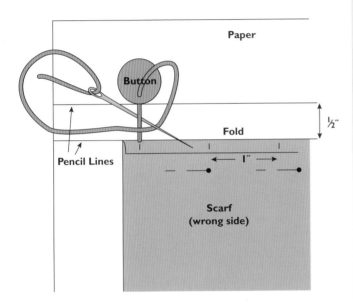

Attach felted buttons to hem with knots.

9. Reinsert the needle into the same mark at folded edge. Knot thread under fold to secure. Carry the needle inside fold and draw it out at the next mark. Add the next felted button and knot as before (Step 8). Continue until 7 buttons are attached to the edge. Repeat Steps 6–9 to fringe other short edge of scarf.

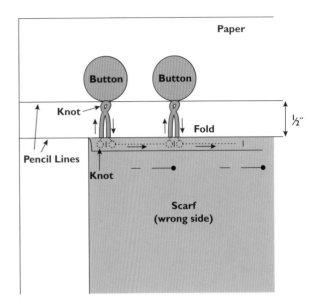

Secure felted buttons to hemline.

10. Using matching sewing thread, hand stitch the folded edge into place to finish hem.

 Use cookie cutters to needle felt other simple shapes. Try hearts for someone you love or stars on a child-size scarf.

BEADED STRIPES PURSE

by Diane McCauley

Use a recycled sweater, bits of yarn and thread, roving, and a few beads to make a quick-change slipcover for a purse. Shop for a ready-to-embellish purse at your local craft store or online. Choose a simple, flat pocket style, such as the 7″ × 9″ bag we've used here.

SUPPLIES

Ready-to-embellish shoulder bag (Bagworks, Inc.)

Felted sweater (see How to Felt Wool Yardage and Sweaters on page 8)

Wool roving, up to ½ oz. each of three colors

Assorted bits of thread, novelty yarn, and fibers

Beads

2 clip-on strap hooks

Matching sewing thread and needle

Needle felting tools

CUTTING

From felted sweater:

Measure the length and width of the ready-to-embellish purse. Add ¼″ to each measurement. Use measurements to cut two rectangles of equal size.

Cut enough 1½″-wide strips to total 56″ for strap.

INSTRUCTIONS

Refer to Fiber to Fabric on page 8.

1. Place one sweater rectangle on work surface for purse front. Arrange a variety of threads and yarns on the middle of the piece, intertwining and looping them to form a loosely organized vertical stripe. Lay roving over the threads, using small amounts so threads show through. Needle felt layers to anchor the fibers in place. Repeat to add two more stripes.

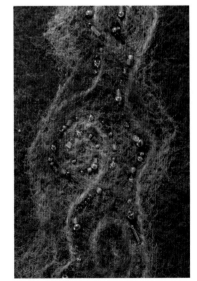

Intertwine and loop yarns and threads to create vertical stripes.

For optional two-sided embellished purse, repeat layering and felting on second sweater rectangle.

tip For a super-simple project, use a striped or patterned sweater as your felted base. Enhance or emphasize the existing pattern with roving or yarn.

2. Sew beads on the stripes, varying the density from widely spaced to tightly clustered. Keep beads ⅜″ from outer edges for seam allowance.

3. Set the sewing machine to a medium zigzag stitch. Place the two rectangles right sides together. Sew around sides and bottom using a ¼″ seam allowance; leave top edge open. Turn right side out, creating an open pocket slipcover.

4. Line up the 1½″ strap strips end to end. Overlap the ends by a few inches and stitch diagonally across overlap through both layers. Stitch again close to the first stitching line, about ⅛″ apart. Trim overlapped strips close to the stitching line on both sides to create diagonal seam. Continue until you have one long strip.

5. Fold the strip in half lengthwise. Stitch ½″ from the folded edge. Trim close to the stitching line. Cut the strip to the desired strap length plus 1½″. Slip each end of the strap through a clip-on hook, fold the ends back onto the strap, and stitch to secure.

Slip strap end through clip-on hook, fold end back, and stitch to secure.

6. Stretch the embellished slipcover over the purchased purse. Slipcover will fit snugly. Clip the strap onto the purse loops.

tip Use other techniques or designs from this book to make an entire wardrobe of quick-change purses and handles.

by Sarah Sporrer

We needle felted into unbleached linen fiber to make this 16″ × 16″ pillow. Experiment with different foundation fabrics—you may find some needle more quickly than others. Different fibers and yarns were used to create the shading on the fern leaves.

SUPPLIES

Yardages are based on 40"-wide fabric (after prewashing).

⅝ yard unbleached linen fabric

¼ yard cotton leaf print

⅝ yard cotton animal print

Wool roving, up to ½ oz. each of five colors: dark green (1), medium green (2), light green (3), dark brown (4), medium brown (5)

Dark green yarn

2 yards cotton cording, ⅛" to ½"

Matching or neutral sewing thread and needle

16" pillow form

Tailor's chalk

Needle felting tools

CUTTING

From unbleached linen, cut:
1 foundation, 9¾" × 12½"

1 background, 17" × 17"

From cotton leaf print, cut:
2 strips 2"; subcut to make:

> 1 inner border, 2" × 12½" (A)

> 1 inner border, 2" × 11¼" (B)

> 1 inner border, 2" × 14" (C)

> 1 inner border, 2" × 12¾" (D)

From cotton animal print, cut:
1 backing, 17" × 17"

1 square, 14" × 14"; subcut into 2"-wide bias strips

INSTRUCTIONS

Refer to Yarn Embellishment on page 7 and Fiber to Fabric on page 8.

1. With chalk, trace fern pattern (page 74) on foundation. Needle felt roving to foundation, following the pattern color guide for shading leaves. Place yarn over traced stem and needle felt in place.

Needle felt roving to background to created shaded leaves.

2. Using a ¼" seam allowance and pressing toward borders, sew inner border A to left side of felted foundation. Sew border B to top edge, border C to right edge, and border D to bottom edge. Press toward border. Turn border under ¼" around outside edges. Press.

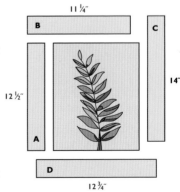

Attach borders to felted foundation.

3. Center the bordered project onto 17″ × 17″ background. Pin. With matching thread, slipstitch folded edge of border to background on all sides to complete pillow front.

4. Sew 2″ bias strips together, end to end, to make one strip 2 yards long. Fold the strip over cotton cording and stitch with a zipper foot to make piping.

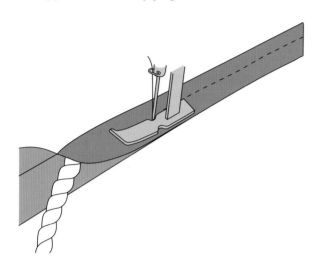

Use a zipper foot to make piping.

5. Using a zipper foot and long stitches, baste piping to pillow front, raw edges matching. Tuck cording ends into fold.

6. Lay pillow front on 17″ × 17″ backing, right sides facing, aligning raw edges. Pin. Use a zipper foot to sew layers together, keeping stitches close to piping and leaving a 3″ opening. Turn pillow right side out. If necessary, remove piping basting stitches. Insert pillow form through the opening and slipstitch closed.

Wool from Scratch

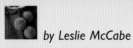 *by Leslie McCabe*

We needle felted the cherries and leaves by hand. This project is quick and easy!

SUPPLIES

Small quantities of wool roving; red in 2 shades, green in 2 shades, brown

Three 1˝ Styrofoam balls

Pin back

#5 perle cotton, brown

Embroidery needle, size #22

Needle felting tools

INSTRUCTIONS

Refer to Wool from Scratch on page 9.

1. Loosely needle some red roving into a freeform square or circle, about 2½˝ across. Layer more tufts of red roving horizontally. Then add roving vertically. Needle to form a smooth piece of felt. Note: Two reds needled together give depth of color; use one or two shades, as desired.

2. Wrap red felt around a Styrofoam ball. Needle until the formed felt is firm and round and the Styrofoam is broken down. In thin areas add more roving and felt in place as needed.

Wrap felted roving around Styrofoam ball and needle until firm.

3. Loosely needle some light green roving into a freeform rectangle about 1½˝ × 3˝. When felting begins, add some darker green roving for shading. Continue needling, folding in the ends to form a leaf shape that is pointed at both ends. Work in a green strand of roving through the center of leaf for veins. Continue needling until the piece is firm and felted.

Form a leaf from a freeform rectangle of roving.

4. Pinch the leaf at the middle and needle into the sides to form two leaves.

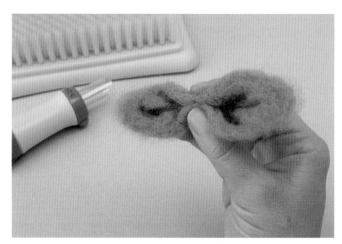

Pinch leaves in the middle to form two leaves.

5. Roll a large tuft of brown roving in your palms, as if rolling clay, creating a snake shape. Place snake on work surface and needle to form a thick, firm twig, about 3″ long. Needle the twin leaves onto the twig. Sew a pin back to the back of the twig.

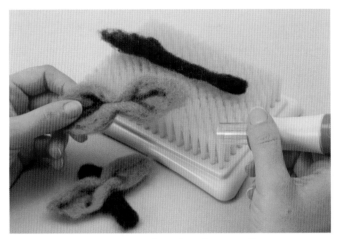

Roll large tufts of roving and needle to form firm twigs. Use one twig with twin leaves per pin.

6. Thread an embroidery needle with brown perle cotton. Sew in and out of a felted cherry, as shown, to create a stem and then stitch the stem to the twig. Repeat for each cherry, varying the stem length.

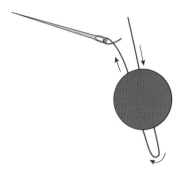

Sew perle cotton through cherry to create stem.

by Leslie McCabe

The challenge of this project is to form a three-dimensional shape as you needle. Work the needle at an angle to add more thickness where you want it. Your flowers will take shape before your eyes.

SUPPLIES

Small quantities of wool roving in six colors: red, gold, green, green-gold, brown, black

Grosgrain ribbon, two 5″ lengths

Matching thread and needle

Awl or tapestry needle

Needle felting tools

INSTRUCTIONS

Refer to Wool from Scratch on page 9.

1. Needle felt tufts of gold or red roving into a 3″ circle (for a small flower). Using an awl or tapestry needle, bring the outer edge in toward the center of the circle to form the edge of a petal. At the same time, continue needling with other hand to hold the shape. Repeat around circle to form four or five evenly spaced petals.

Needle felt tufts of roving into 3″ circles. Use an awl or tapestry needle to bring outer edge toward center to create petal.

2. Flip the flower over on the work surface and needle other side. Hold your needle at an angle and go in between the petals to add shape and thickness to the flower. Work from side to side until the small flower is completely formed and firm.

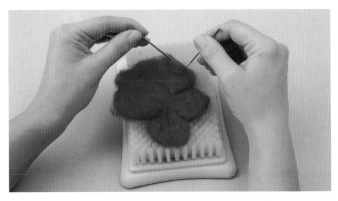

Work the needle at an angle to add more thickness.

3. Repeat Steps 1 and 2 to make two or three small 4- or 5-petal flowers.

4. Repeat Steps 1 and 2, starting with a 4″ circle of roving, to make two or three large flowers.

5. Roll a small tuft of brown roving into a small marble-size ball. Needle it into the center of a flower until it flattens slightly. Roll a smaller ball of black roving and needle it onto the flattened brown roving. Repeat for each flower.

6. Loosely needle some green roving into a freeform rectangle about $1^{1}/_{4}″ \times 2^{1}/_{2}″$. Pull down a corner of the rectangle with an awl or tapestry needle. At the same time, continue needling with other hand. Repeat at each corner to form a pointed leaf shape. Roll small tufts of green-gold roving for the spots, place them on the leaf, and needle felt in place. Make 2 leaves.

7. Roll tufts of green roving between your palms to form a snake. Needle the snake to make a strong, firm piece about 5″ long and $^{1}/_{2}″$ in diameter for the bracelet foundation. Arrange the flowers and leaves on the foundation and needle until firmly attached.

Arrange felted flowers and leaves onto 5″ long felted snake; needle until firmly attached.

8. Sew a 5″ length of grosgrain ribbon to each end of the snake foundation. Attach bracelet to wrist with ribbon.

 tip For a bangle bracelet, start with a larger roving snake. Needle felt the snake ends together to form a circle. Attach flowers to the circular snake to form bangle.

by Amy Barickman

We needle felted the decorations on the orange pocket front of this card case
by hand. We switched to machine felting to attach the pocket to the green back.
Machine needle felting is more aggressive and allows us to secure felt pieces
quickly and efficiently.

SUPPLIES

Scrap wool felt, $5\frac{1}{2}'' \times 5''$, green

Small quantity of wool roving, orange

1 yard yarn, green

$\frac{5}{8}''$ button

Matching sewing thread and needle

Needle felting tools

INSTRUCTIONS

Refer to Wool from Scratch on page 9.

1. Needle felt roving into a $4'' \times 4\frac{3}{4}''$ piece of felt. Hold it up to the light to check thickness, adding more roving, if necessary, so no light penetrates. The edges will not be perfectly straight, which adds interest.

2. Arrange a 10″ piece of yarn into a swirl centered on the felted piece of roving. Needle felt in place. Dampen the piece in warm, soapy water to further bond the fibers, creating the pocket front.

Arrange and needle felt yarn into a swirl design.

3. Cut a 16″ piece of yarn and fold it in half. Tie a knot 1″ from the folded end to form a loop. Twist yarn tail ends together, then center on $5\frac{1}{2}'' \times 5''$ wool felt piece, so loop extends beyond one short edge. Needle felt yarn to secure, creating the card case back.

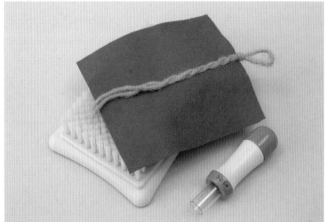

Center yarn loop on card case, twist yarn, and felt in place.

4. Place pocket front on bottom edge of card case back, wrong sides together, allowing a $\frac{1}{8}''$ to $\frac{1}{4}''$ border along side and bottom edges. Yarn loop should be at same end as pocket opening. Needle felt side and bottom edges of pocket front to card case back, leaving top edge open to form a pocket. Make sure pocket front is securely attached.

Join the pocket front to the card case back.

5. Fold the looped end of card case back onto pocket front to form a flap. Gently stretch and pull the flap to soften the edge. Sew a button to pocket front over swirl design.

WOVEN COASTERS

by Amy Barickman

Experiment with different yarns, such as angora or silky fibers, for this plaid technique—they all felt differently. Our coasters showcase mohair fiber, which gives an airy, fuzzy look.

SUPPLIES

Wool roving, up to ½ oz. each, in 3 coordinating colors

Scissors

Needle felting tools

INSTRUCTIONS

Refer to Wool from Scratch on page 9.

1. Needle felt one color of roving into a 5″ × 5″ foundation piece, or a little larger than the desired finished coaster size. Occasionally pull the work away from work surface to check and needle felt back side. Keep needling, flipping the work often, to create a smooth, firm foundation.

2. Select small amounts of roving in two coordinating colors. Roll fibers between your palms to create two or three snakes from each color, about 5″ long.

3. Weave roving snakes in an over-under pattern on top of coaster foundation. Needle felt through all the layers to secure woven roving.

4. Use scissors to square up edges and trim the coaster into the desired shape.

 This weaving technique is a simple yet striking way to combine color. Try it for creating home décor (pillows and table mats) or wearables (embellished scarfs, handbags, or clothing).

Weave rolled fibers to create pattern.

 by Diane McCauley

There are no quilting cottons in this striking wallhanging. It is made of needle felted wool and assorted fibers. Cutting and rearranging a single piece of needle felted fabric makes for a surprisingly complex design. Don't let the instructions intimidate you—once you get the piecing sequence, it is really quite simple to accomplish. Our designer felted this project by machine. The finished piece measures 26″ × 30″.

SUPPLIES

1 yard red-violet wool fabric, 60″ wide

Wool roving, up to ½ oz. each of four colors: medium steel blue, dusty peach, rosy red, medium red-violet

Assorted novelty yarns and threads

⅔ yard Lite Steam-a-Seam 2 fusible web, 18″ wide

Masking tape

Canvas stretcher bars

Rotary cutter, ruler, and mat

Tailor's chalk

Needle felting tools

CUTTING

From wool fabric, cut:

1 foundation, 15″ × 19″

1 backing, 26″ × 30″

INSTRUCTIONS

Refer to Wool from Scratch on page 9.

1. With chalk, mark curving lines on the 15″ × 19″ foundation, dividing it roughly into quarters. Lay assorted yarns and threads on the piece and use the marked lines as a guide to form graceful curves and loops.

2. Add roving to the piece, working freely and quickly, placing broad sweeping curves, swaths, or spirals of color. Let one color predominate in each quadrant but include small amounts of the other colors for a pleasing balance in color, pattern, and texture. Allow some of the felt foundation to show through. Needle felt to secure layers to foundation.

 tip Approach this project with a sense of adventure and experimentation. No matter what you do, the results will be surprising and exciting.

3. Apply fusible web to the back of the felted foundation, following the manufacturer's directions. Leave backing paper on foundation.

4. Use a rotary cutter to trim ½″ off each edge, or enough so that the piece measures 14″ × 18″. Place the piece lengthwise on work table, and cut in half vertically. Starting from center, cut each half into 5 strips that are increasingly wider as you near the outer edge. Make your narrowest strip no less than ½″ wide and your widest strip no more than 3″ wide. Cut 10 strips total.

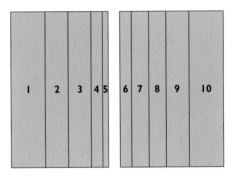

Cut each half into 5 strips that are increasingly wider toward outer edges.

5. Rearrange the order of the strips to mix things up. Be creative, place narrow strips next to wide strips, and wide strips next to medium strips until a pleasing array is designed. Or refer to the illustration below for specific strip placement.

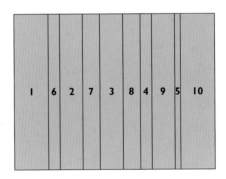

Rearrange strips to mix things up.

6. One strip at a time, peel off fusible web backing paper and reposition strips horizontally on the cutting mat in the same order. As in Step 4, cut the strips in half vertically. Then cut each half into 4 strips that are increasingly wider as you near the outer edge, forming rectangular pieces. Apply masking tape to the top surface of each vertical row to keep the pieces together and in order.

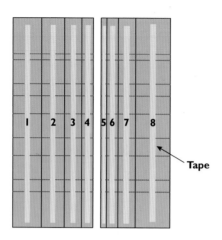

Cut each half into 4 strips that are increasingly wider toward outer edges.

7. Carefully lift each taped row from the cutting mat and rearrange them, intermixing wide, medium, and narrow rows into a pleasing array or use the illustration for exact placement option. Replace any segments that dislodge from the tape.

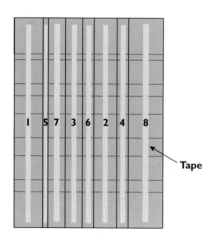

Rearrange the taped rows.

8. Transfer the rows in order onto the 26″ × 30″ wool backing, allowing a 5″ to 6″ border all around the outside edge. Straighten the rows, butting the pieces closely together, and pin in place. Carefully remove the masking tape. Fuse the pieces to the wool backing one row at a time.

9. Needle felt the edges of each horizontal and vertical row by machine to permanently anchor the pieces in place. The more you needle felt the row intersections, the more defined the segments will become. Needle felt lightly if you want a uniform look, more heavily if you want the individual segments to stand out.

10. Mount the finished piece on canvas stretcher bars for display.

> **tip** For a more comprehensive explanation of this technique and many more intriguing ideas, consult *Ricky Tims' Convergence Quilts* (C&T Publishing, 2000).

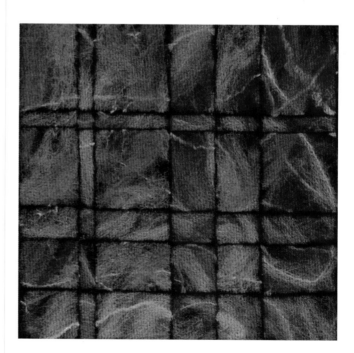

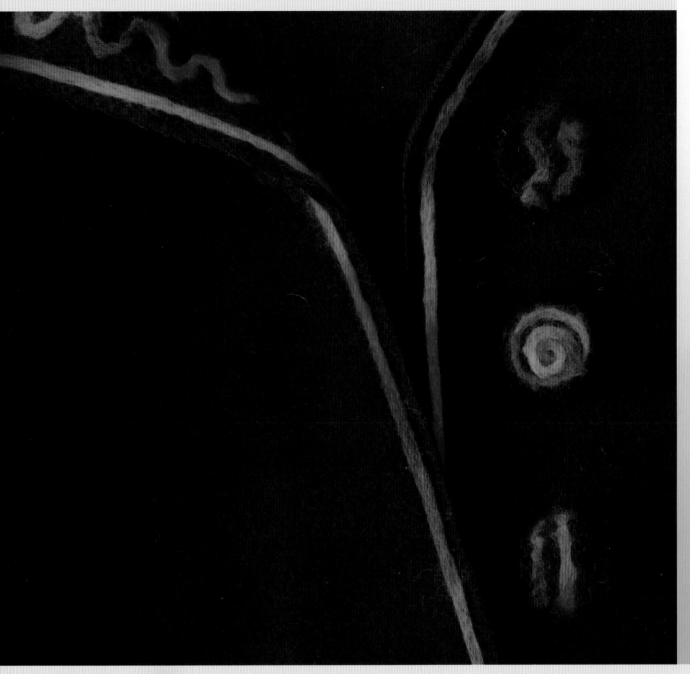

 by Diane McCauley

Want buttons to *exactly* match that needle felted garment or purse? Make your own! Needle felted buttons are somewhat pliable, but still functional. If you want a slightly firmer, more durable button, take this idea a step further and wet felt a custom button with a little soap and hot water. Select a small cookie or canapé cutter in the desired shape and near in size or a little larger than the finished button.

SUPPLIES

Wool roving in one or more colors

Small quantity of wool yarn, roving, or other fibers for embellishment

Small cookie or canapé cutter

Small shank button with a flat top or glue-on button back (Waechter's Silk Shop)

Embellishment glue (Aleene's Jewel-It)

Needle felting tools

INSTRUCTIONS

Refer to Fiber to Fabric on page 8 and Wool from Scratch on page 9.

Dry Needle Felting

Add embellishment to dry felted buttons

1. Place the cookie cutter directly on the work surface and fill it with wool roving. Hold the needle vertically against the inner edge of the cutter. Needle felt around the cutter edge to define the shape, then felt from the edge toward the center.

2. Remove the cookie cutter and pull the button from the work surface. Turn the button over and insert it back into the cutter. Add more roving and repeat the felting technique from Step 1. Continue turning and adding fiber until the button is approximately $1\frac{1}{2}$ times the desired depth.

3. Add bits of contrasting roving, yarns, or other fibers topped with a bit of roving. Needle felt the embellishments to secure them in place.

4. Use repeated shallow stabbing strokes to firm and compress the fibers.

5. Remove the button from the cookie cutter. Make short stabbing strokes around the perimeter of the button, holding the needle parallel to or at a slight angle to the face of the button. Continue until the edges are smooth and the button is firm.

6. Glue a button back or a small shank button to the back of the felted button. Let dry thoroughly.

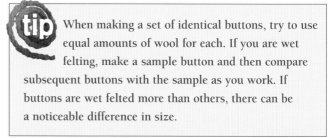

tip When making a set of identical buttons, try to use equal amounts of wool for each. If you are wet felting, make a sample button and then compare subsequent buttons with the sample as you work. If buttons are wet felted more than others, there can be a noticeable difference in size.

Wet Felting

Use hot, soapy water for wet felted buttons

1. Follow Dry Needle Felting Steps 1–3 to start the button.

2. Remove the button from the cookie cutter and dip it in very hot, soapy water (dishwashing liquid works well). Hold the button flat between your thumb and forefinger. With your other thumb and forefinger, press the edges toward the center. Periodically dip the button into the hot water and add more soap to keep the button warm and slippery. Continue to move your fingers around the button until you feel the edges thickening and starting to firm.

3. Place the button in the palm of your hand. Gently rub it between your palms two or three times. Turn the button 90 degrees and rub it between your palms again. Check the results. If the edges have thinned, repeat Step 2. Alternate between Steps 2 and 3 until the button is firm and smooth.

4. Rinse the button well in clean water. Press in a towel to remove excess moisture. Allow to completely dry. Glue a button back or a small shank button to the back of the felted button. Let glue dry thoroughly.

Wet or Dry?

Our designer recommends wet felted buttons for heavier wear and for garments that require firmer, smoother buttons. On garments that are worn infrequently, either wet or dry felted buttons should hold up fine. With either method, make a sample button to see whether you are satisfied with the results. Wools vary on how firmly they needle felt and how much they shrink when wet felted.

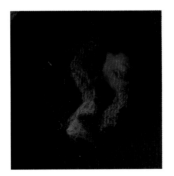

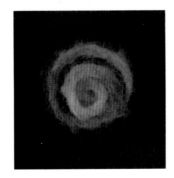

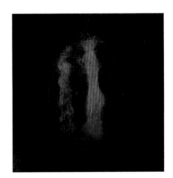

DAYLILY PIN

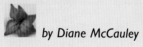

by Diane McCauley

Three colors of wool blend together to give this delicate daylily pin a lifelike look. It measures about 5″ across, and its resemblance to a real flower is stunning. Our designer did the original pin by machine, but she tried a sample petal by hand and that method worked equally well.

SUPPLIES

Wool roving, up to ½ oz. each of three or more colors

Tapestry wool or other fine wool yarn in matching color, 24″ long

Water-soluble stabilizer, 8″ × 16″ (Sulky Super Solvy Heavier Water Soluble Stabilizer)

24-gauge craft wire

Artificial daylily stamens *or* 22-gauge wire, four ¼″ oval beads, and red paint or nail polish

Craft glue that dries clear

Scrap of green felt

Sew-on pin back

Permanent marker

Matching sewing thread and needle

Awl or tapestry needle (optional)

Needle felting tools

INSTRUCTIONS

Refer to Fiber to Fabric on page 8 and Wool from Scratch on page 9.

1. Cut the stabilizer into two 8″ squares. With permanent marker, trace the base petals pattern (page 75) on one square and the top petals pattern (page 75) on the other square.

2. Use the traced pattern as a guide; start at the outer edges and needle felt roving to the stabilizer. Use enough wool to fully cover the stabilizer, but avoid a heavy buildup, keeping the petals light and delicate. As you move toward the center of a petal, add a splash of contrasting color as noted on the pattern. Needle felt a length of yarn for a vein down the center of each petal. Repeat to make one top petal unit and one base petal unit.

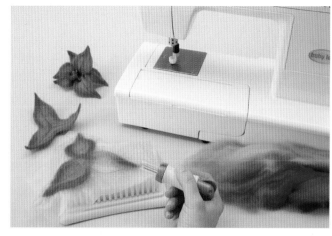

Needle felt roving to stabilizer.

3. Trim petals from stabilizer along the pattern line. If any stabilizer shows after trimming, moisten to dissolve it. Leave the remaining stabilizer in place.

4. Cut a length of 24-gauge craft wire to extend from the tip to the center of each petal. Glue the wire to the reverse side of each petal. Cover the glued areas with foil and weight with a book until the glue is dry.

5. Layer the top petal unit on the base petal unit, offsetting the petal points. Tack the layers together with a few hand stitches at the center. Then turn the felted flower upside down and pinch into shape. Make a tuck at the base of each petal and pull the stitches tight to define the flower.

6. Insert the stamens (see How to Make Stamens on page 62), using an awl or tapestry needle to make a hole, if needed. Cut the wire approximately ¼″ beyond the base of the flower, and bend up the wire ends. Arrange the stamens. Add a drop of glue at the base of the flower to hold stamens in place. Cut the stem pattern (page 75) from green felt. Glue the stem to the base of the flower to hide the wires.

7. Sew a pin back to the stem on the back of the flower.

 tip Consult garden catalogs for other floral shapes that can be translated into wool felting. Try an orchid, a pansy, or an anemone or capture the vivid colors of fall with a cluster of leaves. Water-soluble stabilizer gives you the opportunity to make freestanding shapes that can be quite delicate or, with more wool, quite lush.

How to Make Stamens

Cut a 4″ length of 22-gauge wire. Form a tiny loop at one end. Thread an oval bead on the wire and slide it to the loop. Bend the wire at a 90° angle at the base of the bead. Color the wire and bead with paint or nail polish.

Thread bead on wire loop to make stamens.

FLOWER PIN by Barbara Lambrecht

Gallery

SOUTHWEST SWIRL CLUTCH PURSE
by Barbara Lambrecht

FRUIT SALAD SALSA EVENING BAG
by Barbara Lambrecht

BALLS by Suzanne Higgs

BURGUNDY VESSEL by Suzanne Higgs

SUNSET DELIGHTS PURSE by Barbara Lambrecht

GRAY VESSEL (WET FELTED) by Suzanne Higgs

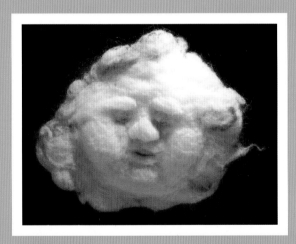

CLOUD FACE by Suzanne Higgs

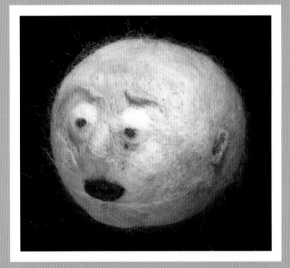

MOON FACE by Suzanne Higgs

BLUE HAT (WET FELTED)
by Suzanne Higgs

BLACK & FUCHSIA PURSE
by Diane McCauley

BLACK & FUCHSIA COLLAR
by Diane McCauley

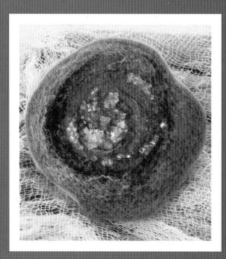

GEODE PIN by Diane McCauley

CAST-OFF HANDBAG
by Diane McCauley

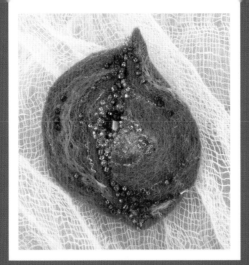

AZURE PIN by Diane McCauley

LILY PURSE by Diane McCauley

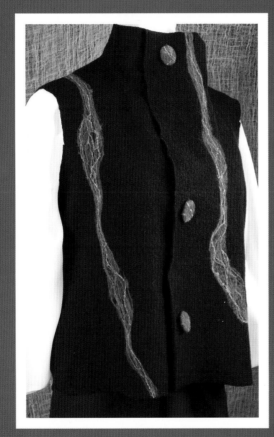

TACTILE WAVES VEST by Diane McCauley

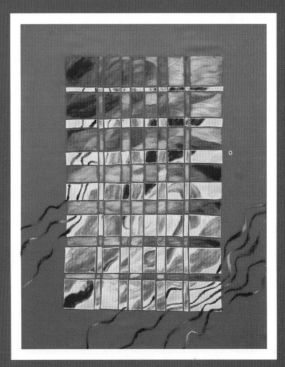

TRIAD WALLHANGING by Diane McCauley

ARIEL'S POUCH (WET FELTED)
by Diane McCauley

TIGER LILY PIN
by Leslie McCabe

SHEEP FARMER'S PINCUSHION
by Michele DuPont Mangham

PINK TULIPS
by Sarah Sporrer

LADYBUG PIN
Leslie McCabe

BRACELET BALLS
by Leslie McCabe

JEANS
by Leslie McCabe

PENDANT
by Leslie McCabe

EASY SILHOUETTE VEST
by Mary Ann Donze

ENVELOPE CLUTCH
by Amy Barickman

BUTTON BAND
by Amy Barickman

SHORT FLORAL SWIRL SCARF
by Amy Barickman

UPTOWN COLLAR
by Diane McCauley

Patterns

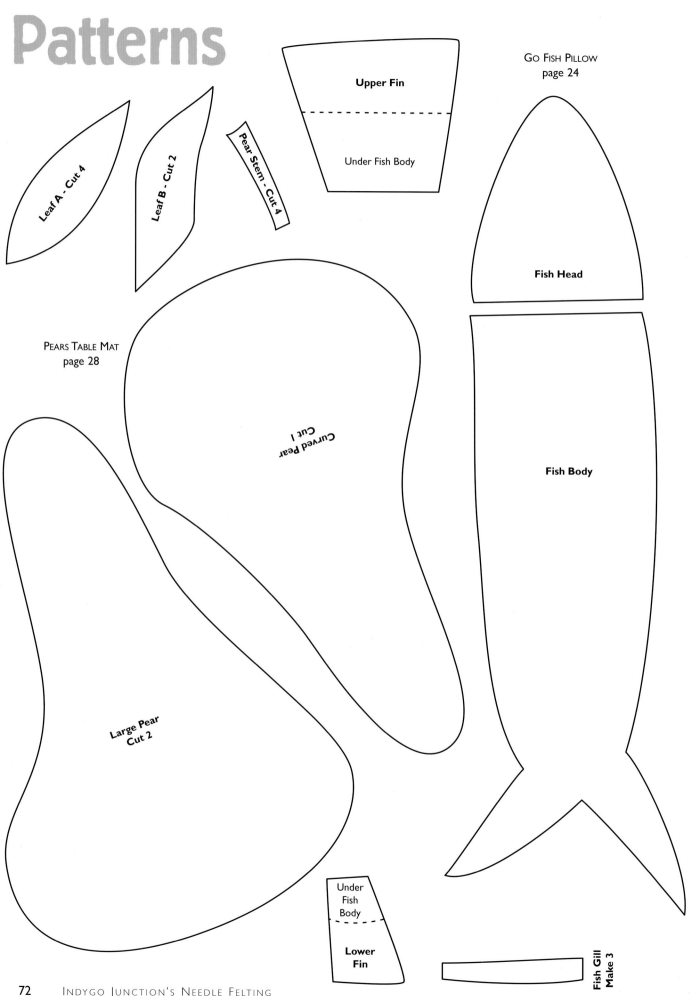

Leaf A - Cut 4

Leaf B - Cut 2

Pear Stem - Cut 4

Upper Fin

Under Fish Body

Go Fish Pillow
page 24

Fish Head

Pears Table Mat
page 28

Curved Pear
Cut 1

Fish Body

**Large Pear
Cut 2**

Under
Fish
Body

**Lower
Fin**

Fish Gill
Make 3

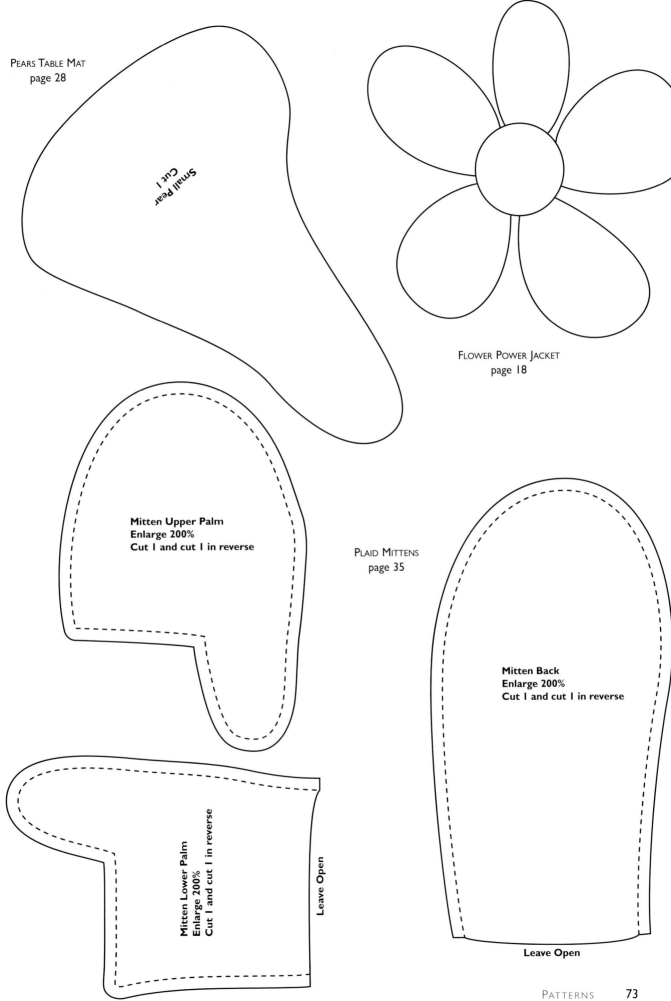

PEARS TABLE MAT
page 28

Small Pear
Cut 1

FLOWER POWER JACKET
page 18

**Mitten Upper Palm
Enlarge 200%
Cut 1 and cut 1 in reverse**

PLAID MITTENS
page 35

**Mitten Back
Enlarge 200%
Cut 1 and cut 1 in reverse**

**Mitten Lower Palm
Enlarge 200%
Cut 1 and cut 1 in reverse**

Leave Open

Leave Open

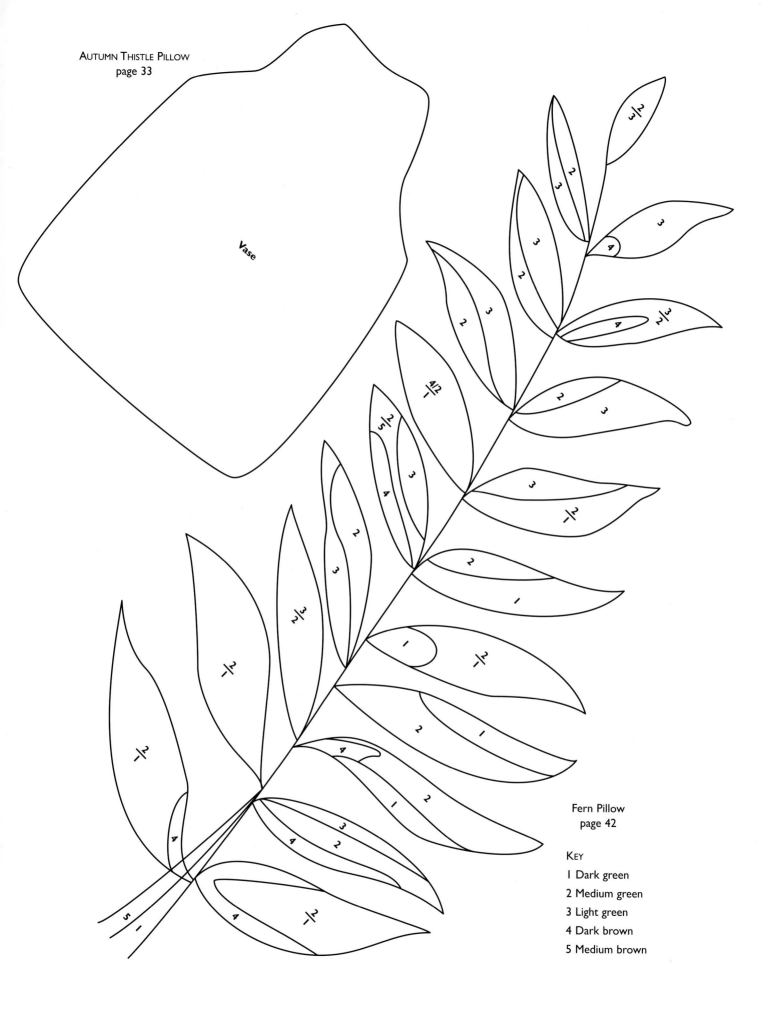

Autumn Thistle Pillow
page 33

Vase

Fern Pillow
page 42

Key
1 Dark green
2 Medium green
3 Light green
4 Dark brown
5 Medium brown

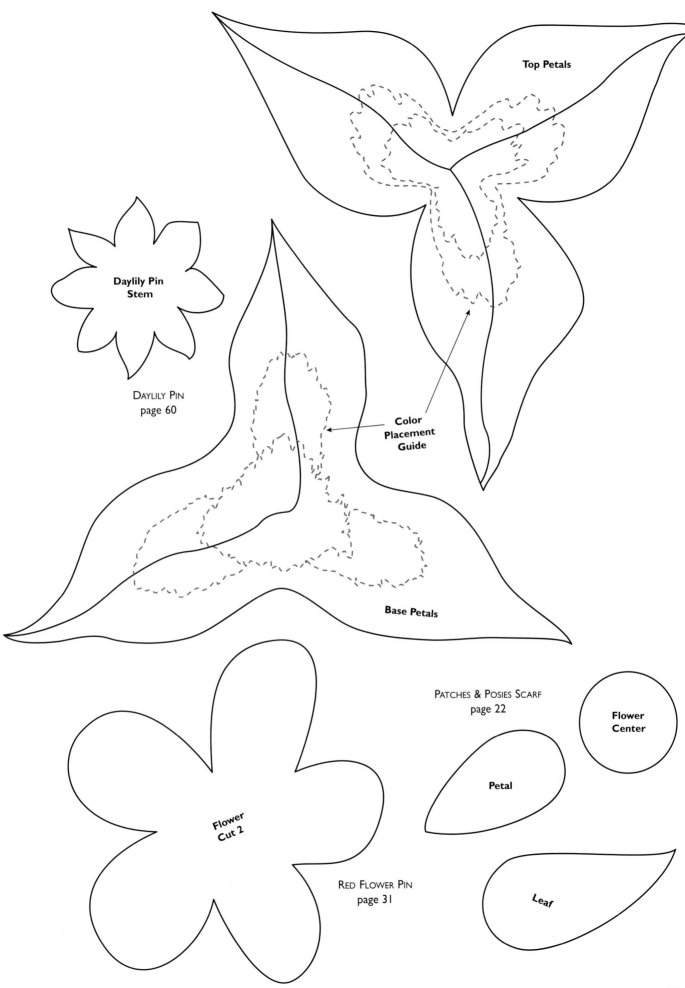

Top Petals

Daylily Pin Stem

DAYLILY PIN
page 60

Color
Placement
Guide

Base Petals

PATCHES & POSIES SCARF
page 22

**Flower
Center**

**Flower
Cut 2**

Petal

RED FLOWER PIN
page 31

Leaf

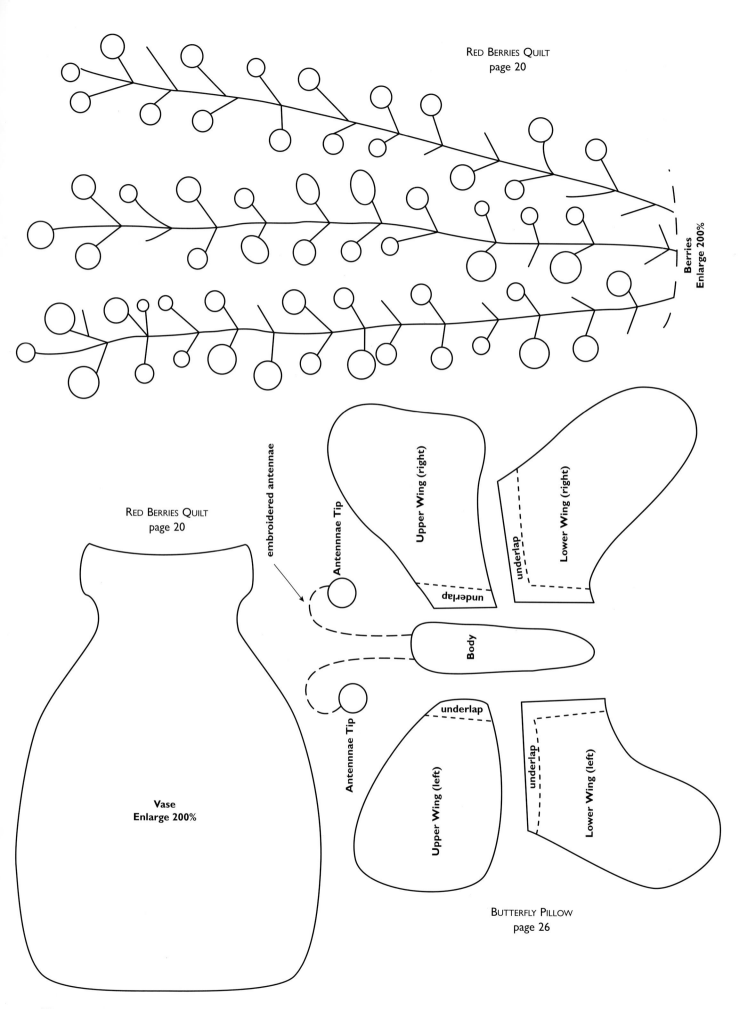

RED BERRIES QUILT
page 20

Berries
Enlarge 200%

RED BERRIES QUILT
page 20

embroidered antennae

Antennnae Tip

Upper Wing (right)

Lower Wing (right)

underlap

underlap

Body

Vase
Enlarge 200%

Antennnae Tip

underlap

Upper Wing (left)

underlap

Lower Wing (left)

BUTTERFLY PILLOW
page 26

RESOURCES

Tools, kits, fabric, fiber, supplies, and accessories

INDYGO JUNCTION, INC.

Amy Barickman (owner/designer)

P.O. Box 30238

Kansas City, MO 64112

(913)-341-5559

www.indygojunctioninc.com or www.thevintagework-shop.com

ALEENE'S JEWEL-IT

Available at craft stores

BABYLOCK EMBELLISHER

Available through Babylock retailers

www.babylock.com

BERNAT YARNS

Available at fine yarn and fabric stores

www.bernat.com

BAGWORKS, INC.

3301-C South Cravens Road

Ft. Worth, TX 76119

817-446-8080 or 800-365-7423

www.bagworks.com

CASCADE YARNS

Available at fine yarn and fabric stores

www.cascadeyarns.com

CLOVER FELTING PUNCH TOOL AND MAT

Available at fine yarn and craft stores

Clover Needlecraft, Inc.: www.clover-usa.com

HEAVY INTERFACING

Peltex Extra Firm by Pellon

Timtex by Timber Lane Press

Available in the interfacing section of fine fabric stores

HOOKED ON FELT

Suzanne Higgs (owner/designer)

269-685-7077

www.hookedonfelt.com

LITE STEAM-A-SEAM 2 FUSIBLE ADHESIVE

Available in the interfacing section of fine fabric stores

The Warm Company: www.warmcompany.com

MARCUS BROTHERS TEXTILES, INC.

Available at fine fabric stores

www.marcusbrothers.com

MANGHAM MANOR

Michele Mangham (owner/designer)

434-973-2222

www.wool.us

NATIONAL NONWOVENS

Available at fine fabric and craft stores

www.nationalnonwovens.com

SULKY SUPER SOLVY HEAVIER WATER SOLUBLE STABILIZER

Available in the interfacing section of fine fabric stores

Sulky of America – www.sulky.com

UNITED NOTIONS/MODA FABRICS

Available at fine fabric stores

www.modafabrics.com

WAECHTER'S SILK SHOP

www.waechters.com

WEEKS DYE WORKS

Available at fine yarn, fabric, and craft stores

www.weeksdyeworks.com

About the Author

Amy Barickman, founder and owner of Indygo Junction, Inc., and The Vintage Workshop, grew up in the retail crafting business and is today a leader in the quilt and clothing pattern craft industry. She started Indygo Junction in 1990 to showcase the talent of leading craft designers. Amy's knack for anticipating popular styles and trends has helped her discover and mentor fresh, new design talent. To date, she has worked with more than 25 artists, guiding them, through a unique partnership, to create with innovative materials. She began The Vintage Workshop in 2002 to create products that combine the timeless beauty of vintage artwork with the remarkable accessibility of the computer and inkjet printable materials. In *Indygo Junction's Needle Felting*, Amy has once again brought together a group of talented designers and introduced them to the fabulous crafting technique of needle felting. The resulting projects boast Indygo Junction's sophisticated style signature . . . *handmade style for the creative spirit.*

Great Titles from C&T PUBLISHING